BEYOND THE EQUATOR

GOOD TO GO 2

JEFFREY VONK

ISBN: 9789493056268 (ebook)

ISBN: 9789493056251 (paperback)

Publisher: Amsterdam Publishers

CONTENTS

This book is dedicated to my daughter
who was never given the chance to breathe her first breath,
and to all of those who have lost a child.
Let's live life to the fullest, every day anew.

INTRODUCTION

The late Wilbur E. Garrett once wrote: "When we try to explain the daredevil behavior of a cat we say 'Curiosity killed the cat' and when it somehow survives we cover that with 'A cat has nine lives'. The same could be said about explorers."

When I ran away from home for the first time I was only three years old. It's actually my very first memory. My dad was a bricklayer but due to a back injury, he spent most of his time as a security guard at a factory, if he wasn't busy volunteering at the fire fighters, so I didn't see him often. Therefore, my mother was usually the one to take my brother and me to school on the bicycle, which is quite common in the Netherlands. Propped against the child seat in the back, I was always absorbing my surroundings with a growing urge to question the unknown, laying a foundation for intrusiveness so to speak.

Back home my mother would return to her daily chores like doing the laundry, which she takes a bit too seriously by even ironing the washcloths. During one of these unguarded, busy moments I saw a chance for my long-anticipated escape. Having crossed the busy traffic-filled street I vanished into forbidden terrain. Young as I was, I still recall the euphoria of nobody looking over my shoulder or correcting me. I wasn't put on this earth to live like a bird in a cage; somehow, there has always been the need to break free. Turns out the good Lord had blessed me with a photographic memory and I ended up following the same path to the elementary school my older brother went to. From my bicycle seat, I had memorized the entire route whilst figuring out a shortcut with my built-in compass. However, I was presented with a small challenge. In those days, the municipality was digging a huge canal straight through the village establishing new suburbs. Builders had left a timber beam across the still dry canal at a height of about six yards.

Step-by-step my little feet slide forward, the muddy bottom ready to gorge my tiny existence. When the timber starts to tremble, I hesitate for a second. Quickly overcoming my anxiety, I finally reach the other side. While relishing in this personal triumph my poor mother is wiping the sweat from her brow. Where can her little boy be? He's nowhere to be found. Expecting the worst, hastened feet stride to the dike to see whether I'm floating face-down in the lake, or drowned in one of the many surrounding watery trenches. Neighbors notice her state of panic and within minutes the whole block is searching along with my mother. The fear of any parent became a reality for her – her toddler was missing!

Many fretful hours pass until teachers at the elementary school notice an unfamiliar whipper-snapper contentedly minding his own business in the sandpit. Convinced of my innocence I was reunited with the home front later that day. I suppose it's fair to say that it has always been in my blood and this independent mission was the genesis of many more to come.

I am sure you have seen them, those guys with patches of flags of all the countries they have visited sewn onto their bags. Of course, backpacking is not necessarily a new thing. These days, expanding your opportunities is rather the thing to do in a world that is getting smaller and smaller – perhaps now more than ever. The popularity of backpacking has increased thanks to slick travel magazines and a surplus of flashy television programs. Also, let us not forget that due to social media, outdoor stores have seen their net revenues doubled.

Ever since the number of millennials striving to visit the wonders of the world in record time, in order to fill their travel blogs and Instagram pages, it has skyrocketed. Many youngsters will usually travel as much as they can before rushing back for their master's degree for a discipline they will never get a job for. Still, the need to extricate from the mandated matrix is flourishing. Not to mention the new generation of bracelet-braiding hippies; zoned out on the sidewalks by excessive drug use, trying to make a buck selling those bracelets that were already tacky in the stone age, or playing a few cords on sticker-covered guitars, with uncut strings.

But no judgment here – to each his own. Everyone has their own path to walk. Some of us prefer to look and smell like a homeless person, which I'm not foreign to myself. It's all about letting go of the conventional to unleash that shackled inner self, but what does it really mean to visit another country and ingest an abstract language, eat unknown food and dwell in the midst of a culture with such different habits, morals and values? Surely, hanging out in hostels all day doesn't teach you much of the place.

Friends ask "How is your holiday going?" But make no mistake. To me a holiday is – relaxing or active – being surrounded by comfort and security, having your primary needs within reach. To experience the essence of traveling, or true backpacking if you will, one must think in terms of lacking those primary needs.

How about having ice cold showers for a few months? Do you know what that does to a human body or human spirit? Could you handle not having a good sponge for days on end, being dirty and having stinky clothes? Not knowing where you will sleep at night, if at all, or having to find shelter against the freezing air or a sudden downpour? Are you up for making judgment calls in an unsafe area with potential robbers watching you? In addition, you may also have to deal with a hungry pack of dogs who don't look very friendly. Sometimes, in urban or inhabited areas, you may have to hold number one and number two for hours before finding a bathroom. And once it is found... there is no paper. Furthermore, searching for a decent meal means that sometimes you may have to deal with an empty stomach for hours before finding anything edible.

How do you communicate your desires if no one understands what you're saying? Believe me, in many places locals don't even know the word for 'water' in English. Imagine that situation when you're dying of thirst the whole day. Did your colleagues who asked how the holiday was going think about travel insurance? Or how to deal with a stolen passport? Or how to act when your wallet is empty and no one has heard of an ATM, or where to arrange transport if you're on your own in a remote place? Or how to find gasoline with zero gas stations around for miles and miles, and what the hell are miles anyway when you are used to counting in kilometers? Probably the worst thing for most people is the lack of internet for a while, and by that I'm not talking about a mere couple of hours. Not being able to navigate, make travel plans online or communicate with family and friends can be difficult obstacles to overcome. Another often-neglected issue is the culture shock one experiences when going back home. How do you reintegrate into society when you were subject to such a different lifestyle, or when you simply don't have a home to return to? If you go abroad for weeks, months, or years, only one thing has significantly changed when you come back, and that is you.

Okay, now we're starting to get the hang of it. There are indeed quite a few strings attached to traveling. Having said that, it's clear that no one would go into the wild if the hardships weren't worth it. You can end up being astounded by the beauty of multi-colored mountains sitting 12,000 feet above sea level, dwell in the sheer awe of deserts as far as the eye can see or, a place teeming with wildlife that makes you feel truly one with nature – this is your deserved reward. Who can resist jaw-dropping sunrises over ancient geometrical buildings in overgrown jungles, meeting indigenous people in traditional clothing along the way? Who doesn't dream of white sandy beaches beneath a cloudless sky, indulging in warm temperatures surrounded by coconut-filled palm trees when diving in turquoise lagoons?

Traveling reveals the true meaning of the word *recreation*. If you allow me to speak for most of the others like me, that's exactly why we do it. In addition, the opportunity for experiencing personal growth is unprecedented and the knowledge you gain is a gift for the rest of your life as well as for others along the way, the enjoyment of which becomes an everlasting memory.

On more than one occasion, people have told me that I am on the run. In their minds I'm fleeing from something or at least have certain issues for all this pavement chasing. The truth, which apparently some find hard to understand, is that sometimes I just want to see a country! I have this unquenchable curiosity and undying interest in the unexplored. When I am home for too long, if such a thing exists at all, I get homesick for adventure. Is the longing to learn my drug? Maybe it is, but man do I feel alive while being on the move.

Another figurative vertebral column was strengthened in the year 1992. Having crossed several borders my family and I end up in the vicinity of charming Luxembourg. Still a boy at this point of my life I remember the fresh smells of yellow knee-high grass fields, with the brightness of the midday summer sun making our eyes pinch as I French-kiss a girl for the first time. Although this memory sticks with me as unforgettable, the next event sticks out even more.

Amidst the Ardennes, a rugged yet gorgeous mountain range, the campground where we were staying at facilitated a *nightly dropping*. Meaning they would kick us out of a van in the middle of nowhere where we sat blindfolded, only for us to find our way back to the campground again. Arguably the only adventurous thing my parents ever did, they decide to take my brother and me to join the group which existed of approximately seventy people. Once started we march for hours through dense forest, with only a dynamo torch as our source of light. The brave men walk at the front, unknowingly leading us away from our destination by many miles, and encumbered by testosterone it takes a while before they admit we are utterly lost. Take note, this is in an era well before the invention of smartphones and the like. Increasingly concerned, clammy faces stare at the road map, with many women now seemingly worried for the wellbeing of their children as exhaustion and dehydration seeps in. Just when the threatening night seems to lure us further into the wrong direction, a twelve-year-old lad addresses the men claiming to know the way. "I know exactly where we are!" he says. Being more proud than brave, the men harden their hearts and don't want anything to do with him.

Contrary to feeling like a loner, or an outsider even, it has always been remarkably easy for me to connect with others. It so happened that newly-acquainted friends and I had spent a previous week and a half together continuously scouring the woods. Due to my natural tendency to memorize things, I knew every rock, every bush and every trail like the back of my hand. After a lengthy game of persuasion, they eventually follow my lead with the whole group on my tail. Whether with certainty or doubt, they still follow me, bringing an incredible smile to my face. Maybe more like a smirk. Suddenly I had a voice, something that would never have happened had I chosen to stay at home. Now I had given them hope to make it back to their own beds and be reunited with their loved ones left behind at the campground. All those adults placing their trust into the hands of a child is a feeling I'll never forget. I will likewise never forget the look on the brave men's faces as I safely returned everyone back to civilization. Those humbled looks and proud mouths silenced, I cherish like trophies on the mantelpiece. Forevermore, priceless.

Cliché memes say that life is a book – if you don't travel you only read the first page – and in this case, I will have to agree with that. Once, while working at a disorganized woodpile in the state of

Missouri, I made some cash by dismantling old pallets. Here I asked a Chicago resident if he also liked to barbecue on the lakeside back home, since it was crowded as heck there in the summertime. He replied: "What lake?" In reality, he'd never skipped beyond that first page, therefore missing out on so much splendor. Being over thirty the good man spent his whole life in the city and had never seen Lake Michigan, despite it being right under his nose!

Another question that I often get is: "How do you finance all of this?" People have to understand that it's about priorities and sometimes sacrifices. Going to your favorite restaurant every week is not helping if you want to travel, nor is following the latest, ever-changing fashion trends. As for me, another big money saver is the fact that I don't drink or smoke. Also, I don't care about extravagant houses, cars and all kinds of worldly possessions. I have everything arranged pretty well for the small company I own, being a general contractor, but that's it. These are mere investments to fill the piggy bank. That proverbial piggy bank gets smashed to pieces by the first good idea that pops up to hit the road. Transforming these ideas into actually stuffing my backpack and going is unimaginable for some, yet so easy for me.

I remember seeing my parents' bedroom as a child. Weeks before the start of our summer holiday my mom would already have opened up suitcases on the floor. Accompanied by a long, handwritten checklist, filling them until they almost wouldn't close anymore. Nowadays, I gather my stuff literally an hour before I leave and as far as I know, I have never forgotten anything. Unfortunately, airline or bus companies have lost my luggage quite a few times, and while it's no fun you always find a way to manage. Ultimately, making your dreams come true is what it's all about. I hope that this book will allow you to see how my ideas and dreams became reality. Sometimes a little too close to the matter.

In a no-nonsense, unexaggerated way I tried my best to tell it as it happened. Not only do I have a very good memory but I always keep a journal to maintain track of my travels. These recollections, thoughts and emotions aren't loosely based on events, they *are* actual events that eventually turned into the fine copy you hold in your hands right now. Compare it to a logbook with infotainment. In this volume, you will be treated to stories of my time in South America and a slim slice of North- and Central America.

You may find it easy to understand why most things are still so vivid to me. Hopefully, you develop a chronic itch as I have because there is a lot of beauty out there. But even if traveling never becomes your thing you might enjoy reading about the situations I got myself into and perhaps you may learn a thing or two, or be appalled by a thing or three.

If you decide to give it a try, remember that borders exist to be crossed, and boundaries to be vindicated. Society has convinced itself that a mere two weeks' vacation a year should do the trick, and people accept it as the norm. I don't know about you but I refuse to settle for that mindset. No matter the circumstances, I'm always good to go!

A quick disclaimer here. Let me state that I'm not a huge fan of a thing called *political correctness*. However, by no means is it my intention to offend anyone. Regardless of race, gender, ethnicity, religion or background, I treat everyone the same and all people are of equal value to me. Just so you know! As a way to be inclusive to people across all the continents, measurement units of distances and temperatures are used interchangeably.

1

CANADA

For centuries the local inhabitants are accustomed by the windless crisp air, man and animal alike, over time evolved into withstanding the coldest climates. Even for the bravest among them, finding shelter in these vast territories remains a perpetual challenge. It is hard to say where the sky ends and the confines of land begin. White clouds transmute into undistinguishable yet similar complexioned landscapes, undoubtedly mesmerizing to anyone by its unique pureness.

During wintertime in British Columbia you can't afford to lose concentration on the winding mountain roads. The foothills of dense pine forests, classically robed in snow, are watching from the sideline like spectators at a sporting event. Wide branches are clapping their hands while strong trunks shout encouraging words. A thin layer of ice shields the road's surface, leaving its crystals shimmering by penetrating rays of the low sun, preventing tires from making that recognizable squealing sound, while the out-of-control sports car whirls across it.

Ultimately, the vehicle that my buddy Andrew and I are in, slams into a wooden pole of a fence, dislocating the hood, followed by a nose dive into a ditch. Velocity causes the Ford Neon to jump right out of it, slightly diverting from the edge of one of the many ravines about, having us move deeper through a three-feet high grain field. Tentacles of twisted barbed wire scratches irreversible streaks into the car's bright red polish. After a violent launch, the crooked license plate hits asphalt about fifteen yards ahead. The sudden force of the impact causes the windshield to crack into tiny pieces and the airbags to pop out, providing the sensation of an explosion. Last mentioned comes as no surprise as the lifesaver deploys at approximately 200 mph. It smells like fire immediately! Perhaps even far worse, the side windows shatter into uncountable miniature meteorites, sharply attacking my face from every angle as we keep on spinning. An attempt to use my hands to cover my head for protection was futile. In doing so, every exposed part of skin gets torn by glass. With blood leaking out at once, I am now amped up by adrenaline. While still rolling through the rough field another wooden pole finally brings the unmanageable ride to a halt, ending in the same ditch as before, having made an undesigned u-turn. My friend, who so happens to be a brand new driver, is suffering from the seatbelt forcibly cutting into his shoulder, all the while I frantically try to jack open my door, only to find it stuck, the deep dents prevent it from moving the slightest bit. Alarming smoke rises from under the hood. Will we be able to get out from the vehicle before it either bursts into fire, or before the mantle of snow, covering this sloped hillside, carries us to the nearby gaping cliffs after all?

Who could have foreseen this shocking car accident less than a week ago? At that time, I was waking up in one country to the south, in the United States, under the same tree that I had been waking up under for the past twenty days already. To briefly build a bridge to where I left off in the last chapter of Part 1, this happened in St. Louis in Missouri to be precise, that I was on my way to, to surprise a girl. However, after many agonizing months and a series of very ill considered choices coupled with bad luck had left me broke and homeless, even to the point of having to scout the garbage bins at night to find something edible. That is a case of backpacking gone horribly wrong.

Somewhat close to the museum I am hurled up beneath some damp newspapers to stay warm, failing in the attempt. I figure I am close to the zoo, cause I can actually hear the sea lions bark from there, further hindering my efforts to a much needed sleep. Waking up at five thirty in the morning with a nippy breeze plagued by regret, a layer of dew made me realize I couldn't go on like this.

The situation was dire – old newspapers and dry oak leaves, previously my temporary blanket, now functioned as toilet paper. From out of the shrubs I observed the first runners making their rounds through the park, cleverly avoiding the automatic sprinklers which nourished the surrounding green fields. My image, reflecting in one of the motionless ponds, was discouraging to say the least. I began to believe that the purple bags beneath my eyes even scared away the squirrels. An unpleasant shave, using cold water and no cream, made me somewhat presentable again.

The upper compartment of my backpack held my flight ticket out of the misery, quite literally. The one condition that had allowed me to freely venture and travel for many months in these conquered lands, is the evidence of a pre-purchased flight ticket out of the New World, that I obtained when I was still in Turkey. For once, this forced rule is working to my advantage. With that current situation, being broke and all, I would have never made it out on time and would have rendered myself an illegal alien.

As often, if not always, I was pushing things to the limit and leaving things to the last moment. In fact, I only had one day left before my visa would expire, thus jeopardizing getting possible jail time or even deportation from the country; however that was a risk I was not willing to take.

Threading through the eye of the needle this young wanderer hitchhiked to the nearest deteriorated bus station in a final attempt to escape. My smooth talking and begging to passers-by got me into a Greyhound; this being the infamous domestic bus company with a nation-wide network. Passengers inside look just as worn-out as the bus itself, where presumably ninety-nine percent of them are on welfare. The poor, the outcast, the black sheep, the unsuccessful, those are the ones traveling by Greyhound. In that sense I go pretty unnoticed myself and fit in just fine. On the ride to the airport in Chicago, already getting very nervous about having to board that exterminating aircraft, being scared to death of flying, I convinced myself that fortune favors the brave; the destination of my next flight will have to bring salvation.

With heavy showers from the low overcast, strong tires landed on the runway with certain violence. As the plane reduces speed, so does my heartbeat, relieved to have overcome yet another tempting of fate. No wonder that according to the statistics so many people rob themselves of their lives in the incessantly uninviting weather.

On the other hand, the purest of nature abound should spark some form of revitalization. Right beyond the threshold of Vancouver, there is so much beauty to bestow upon! It is easy to imagine what awe the pioneers of the frontier encountered. Massive inspiring trees with a huge diameter, untouched by the eras of time, having survived the atrocities of the titans in the days of old. Broad arms of the ocean's water extends in every direction with the presence of majestic humpback whales within them, almost divine purity of the breathable air as opposed to the suffocating industrial cities we have today, and gracefully hilled lands that, when the rain does stop and light from the sun finally breaks through, it reveals a blaze of glory, flawless in its perfection.

Chilling amidst the strong green pines at the world famous Capilano Suspension Bridge (stretching one hundred sixty meters), it seemed like a good idea to make use of my resources in this area which were once solely the lands of native peoples, some of their descendants are still settled here.

My small address book whispered the name of my old roommate who lives towards the partially snow-covered Fraser Valley. During our time studying in Israel we hung out together every day, and we knew each other well enough to now still feel comfortable around each other, I assumed. And so it happened while moving along rocky rivers and pitches, a good way off the town of Abbotsford, I headed to my old friend's place. In this neck of the woods it is hard not to notice the difference between farms of Dutch and Punjabi settlers, the difference is nothing less than astounding. Almost needless to say, without any prejudge or generalization, the former European farms are kept neat and orderly, whereas the former far Eastern farms are messy, dirty and full of junk.

Arriving at my friend's residence I found out that he, a clever guy on his way to morph into a history teacher, lives with his mom in a trailer, including the child of his sister who herself moved in with her new boyfriend somewhere else. I get entangled in a situation in which a modern-day reality soap opera could eat their heart out. As if that wasn't enough, the trailer is also located on an Indian Reservation, complete with totem pole and all. Well-known clichés truly come to life, instead of igloos on every street corner or ice hockey pucks soaring by, I do see a lot of empty liquor bottles lying around. Wild raccoons gouge through the bags of trash or snatch away the cat's dinner, footprints of moose can be detected in the dirt by a trained eye, and the occasional presence of bears is established by somewhat sinister scratches from razor sharp claws on cars and wooden porches. You do not want to chance upon those ravenous hairy creatures in breeding season!

As we catch up, I joined my old pal Andrew in his cozy, adjacent outdoor Jacuzzi where we enjoyed the freshly fallen snow and colorful strings of lights as it's almost Christmas. While relaxing in the bubbly hot water, accompanied by a yellow rubber duck, the idea was born to do some traveling together, in fact we decide to make a little road trip.

With his hard-earned savings, he is now the owner of a Ford Neon, his pride and joy. Even before obtaining his recently begotten driver license he had already purchased the car – it was simply waiting to be owned by him. In the next few days we make all necessary preparations. Having filled up the trunk with some supplies and extra clothing we reckon ourselves good to go and ready for our ride.

We relished the few days of mild temperatures caused by a rare phenomenon where tropical winds arrive from the Hawaiian Islands. Not being the first time it happens, local people refer to it as the Pineapple Express. You don't normally travel around Canada in winter for the climate. However, the predominantly cold days visibly intensified as we went further inland. Several inches of snow can come down in only one hour, adding to the already garbed mountains that we pass, rugged in nature.

Following the trail we end up at the viewpoint of Jackass Summit, where we enjoyed a clear outlook over the broad river down below. Its surface filled with giant logs, bobbing through the medium current, sometimes for hundreds of kilometers. They go as far as the United States, where enormous saw factories are their proper destiny, concerning the assiduous lumber industry. When Mack freight lorries aren't crawling by, you can spot wildlife doing just that, for example a lonely fox crossing the road, and if you are lucky, or not so much when they are hungry, you can even spot wolves.

At an Asian-owned roadside diner I'm mildly intrigued by the framed pictures of Hollywood movie stars hanging on the wall, who have visited the place in the past. After a short time seated I am introduced to the domestic delicacy of Poutine. For the first time in my life I taste this dish that basically consists of French fries with melted cheese and gravy. Definitely not my cup of tea. *I'll go for mayonnaise anytime!* I'm thinking to myself, as the white sauce is a tradition in the Netherlands.

Serpentine lanes cutting through white prospects donated a good dose of freedom. The thick inborn fur coats of the herds of buffalo, dark in complexion, heavily contrasted the banks of snow about. What marvelous creatures! Watching them with their mighty appearance and chiseled posture they leave behind deep footprints, due to their enormous weight. Marching together they snuffle their snouts, their warm condensing breath making consecutive mantles of clouds like smoke arises from incense.

Remaining in awe as we went by, my thoughts drifted off to centuries before, where millions must have inhabited these unspoiled regions. Speaking about drifting off, slim pockets of ice, seemingly tightly hugging the asphalt, desire to be left alone. After having disturbed the peace and stillness of the surrounding area, our incursion has awakened the gods from their sleep, which haven't yet mastered forgiveness nor do they intend to let us go unpunished, in spite of our well-meant actions in this remoteness.

Mean strands of ice cunningly reach into the tires' profile which unexpectedly pull the car, with us in it, off its course. A slight steering adjustment could have settled the deal. Instead the new driver, still somewhat inexperienced to the lurking dangers of life, decides to step on the breaks in full force! Panically trying to correct his clunky move only results in the worst-case scenario. While spinning around, we are catapulted off the road and uncontrollably swirl into the nearest field.

Coming back to how this chapter started, we are now left with blown-up airbags, glass in our skin with blood streaming out of multiple fissures, and the doors won't open. Bewildered from several blasts through the ditch we make a serious effort to crawl out through the openings where the windows used to be. Luckily the smell of smoke stick to mere smells and nothing spontaneously ignites, but with leaking fluids from all kinds of tubes more hazards are creeping up. Lying on our backs in the snowy field we exhale deep sighs of relief, until it dawns on us that we are far away from safety, from home and civilization; we have to come up with a plan and we'd better do it fast.

Having double-checked that our vital signs are somewhat stable, we begin discussing our limited options when suddenly we spot a single house in the distance; our glimmer of hope. Staggering through the rugged wilderness with bruised ribs and sore legs, we end up at the front door. The type of garbage and rubbish in the garden give away that this property belongs to a Native American family.

After ringing the doorbell repeatedly for a few minutes, someone opens up. It is a young Indian girl. She is home alone and quite surprised to see two tall white guys standing there with torn clothes and bloody faces. We politely ask to use her telephone, since we are out of reach of any reception with our cell phones. Presumably being raised to take precaution she is not to be blamed for not trusting us. Closing the door without letting us in she has the illuminated thought to call the police herself, and not the least.

It is at this point in our adventure where we find out that we are stranded in Indian territory, when after a short while non other than the tribal police shows up – the natives actually have their own police force. Except for hook-noses and protruding cheekbones, they are not very convincing. Especially since one of them has blond hair and blue eyes. Still, by all means they are trying hard to be as sullen and disrespectful as possible.

Without asking whether me and my friend are in need of any medical aid, they unkindly request us to fill out endless legislative paperwork. Since the car is total loss we have to wait for Geoff Parnell's tow-service to haul us out of here. Mind you, the catchy company name of this particular individual is one that will stick with us for the rest of our lives, for who is able to withstand the ingenuity of *Tip Top Towing*?

In the interim of our inquisition by the natives, an amicable woman passing by had left a note with her phone number – just in case. Taking advantage of that situation, she receives a call from the tribal police. As a blessing in disguise, she is happy to inform that the victims are more than welcome to stay the night at her house, showcasing a spoonful of that good old Canadian hospitality. With us bestriding into the spotless backseat of the big police vehicle, its blue and red lights on the roof still flickering, the officers sit themselves in their black leather front seats, carefully keeping an eye on every move we make. All this time we are treated as if we were the biggest criminals on earth.

They look as if we personally are to be blamed for the take-over of the Europeans back in the days. But come-on, it was not as if those tribes were not already savagely butchering each other, not to mention the raging wars that were fought between the natives and their conquistadors, as opposed to the whites just stealing the land. That is a bogus theory. Considerably the only reasonable accusation would be their chronic alcohol use, responsible for a lot of abuse and domestic violence passed down from generation to generation. You know, the callow French and British poachers would actually trade booze and liquor for pelts, not knowing how to catch otters and beavers. Can you imagine?

Contributing to this cagey thought process, one of them unexpectedly asks if we still need to take out our left behind belongings from the wreck, before it's towed off to a garage, or even worse, a scrapyard. Perhaps still woozy from the accident I am certainly not with a right mind when I reckon it to be appropriate to pull their leg, answering with a straight face, "No thank you, we'll pick up that dead body in the trunk later!" Andrew turns his startled head with big eyes, those same eyes screaming in fear and bewilderment of how the hell I could make such a reckless comment and risk incarceration by these spitfires!

Only half realizing what I've just done, a terrible silence befalls inside the car. Now all four of us are mutely staring at each other for about ten seconds, but I guarantee you it feels more like ten very uncomfortable minutes instead. Just when I expect them to swiftly pull their guns on us, or at least at any moment handcuff us to safely get out to inspect the wreck, judging from the intense way the officers make eye contact with one another, maybe even using some unknown spiritual form of tribal communication, they look at us one more time and burst out in laughter! Knowing we are just a couple of numbskulls their attitude turns one hundred eighty degrees, thus, the seemingly impenetrable ice is broken.

From that moment on they become friendly and helpful, even interested in our story. An immensely relieved Andrew wonders how in the world I got away with that one. With a big smile the police officers drop us off at the sympathetic lady's home – a brown wooden house on a mound, log cabin style, where smoke from the chimney produces consoling and welcoming aromas.

After a hot shower washes off the black blood, and after removing glass from our skin with borrowed tweezers, we sink into fluffy armchairs. We are graced with a splendid view (through a huge window) across the white valley, decorated with evergreens on its side. Simultaneously we are graced indoors where a steaming plate of delicious macaroni and cheese awaits us. With the first stars appearing in the partially clouded sky, this road trip has come to an end. I am so thankful that years later I still send her and her husband a postcard during Christmas time. What a joy to know such kind folks exist and how wonderful that somehow, when traveling, the right kind of people are brought upon your path. A little bit of love and compassion can truly make all the difference.

From out of the Korean Embassy in downtown Vancouver, high up in one of the many stately skyscrapers, you are treated to a magnificent panorama of the city's horizon. It is here in this minimalistic yet sterile office, a few days after the accident, that Andrew and I find ourselves amongst numerous yellowish skin toned people. Our time to say goodbye has come, since he is about to receive his visa, and set off to Asia to work as a teacher. Parting our ways, I'm left to spending Christmas on East Hastings, one of the most notorious streets in British Columbia. In spite of the local Salvation Army turning down my open application, I am bound to stand in line like the rest of the vagabonds, waiting for a meal at a homeless shelter.

Yes, for some reason I had chosen to spend these cold and lonely holidays together with drug addicts and prostitutes - needless to say not engaging in their activities. Still, after a few days and nights on the hazardous and filthy streets, surrounded by dirty needles, all sorts of extortion and dodgy robberies, I know it is time to move on. Otherwise I might as well have stayed in that park in the US where I was at before. Sometimes you need to give yourself a little push to keep going forward, for in essence, standing still is going backward. Having had enough of the cold, I long for a warmer season in my life, not yet knowing I would later end up in a rollercoaster of contingencies while on the road.

Yet for now having drifted for nearly a year through the Middle East, and North and Central America as well, where all journeys took place overland, I make my way back to a place I once called home.

There, on the reliable flatlands of Holland, invested by the oh so recognizable windmills, cows and tulips, is where new plans begin to take shape. As all great travels do, it starts with a simple idea, a mere thought, or an igniting dream about some remote location. Daring to let your imagination run wild, that step by step becomes a story, and with or without the support from others, become memories not soon forgotten.

2

COSTA RICA

Becoming a more seasoned traveler I sometimes just want to see another country. In the intro you could read that I'm not necessarily fleeing from issues when I go abroad; as people around me more than sporadically speculate. The next rather lengthy trip is definitely one I was going to do anyway, however, this time I'll admit I embarked a little sooner than initially planned. Breaking the shackles of a dysfunctional relationship with a twelve-year-younger ginger was the cause of this. Trust me when I say this was a journey of its own. So here I am standing at the City Hall to write myself out of my country. No registration means no redundant expenses concerning the obligatory health insurance; one of the methods to outsmart the system. The ladies at the reception desk smile when they see from the database that I have done this trick before. All I can do is smile back when they write *emigration to Costa Rica* on the form.

In the city of Leiden, close to a village where I was renting a free-standing farmhouse on the country side, I return my rental car and take a taxi to the train station. I sold my van a few weeks back, a black Mercedes-Benz Vito, which enables me to stay away longer, having more to spend. On account of flight tickets being hundreds of euros cheaper in Germany, I'm on my way to Frankfurt.

Having arrived in the early evening I obtain some almighty cowboy money to be well prepared, cash is a *must* when one travels, a practice I've learned in years prior.

When everyone has long boarded the airplane and awaits the always exhilarating take off, the pilot announces through the speaker that all luggage has to be unloaded and rechecked for some unknown reason. Gotta love aviation. By the time we are good to go and the engines are turned onto full power I am almost shitting myself from fear. To use an understatement I am still no hero when it comes to flying.

Ten very uncomfortable hours later we land on the Caribbean island of the Dominican Republic. During the short layover, sleepy head passengers gaze at each other and to my surprise I notice some adult German men are still sporting a mullet hanging from the back of their necks. It makes me chuckle every time. In my imagination I ask them, "Finding it a little hard to let go of the seventies, aren't we?" since I don't find the courage to actually ask them.

Our next flight is much shorter than the previous one, but pitifully not less scary. Getting close to my final destination I peek out of the window to see a massive thunderstorm in the distance. Due to the darkness of the night, it produces a light show that no rock concert could measure up to. Just beautiful to witness the clouds light up like that, in mid air.

At the luggage retrieval I find my backpack without the wrap that I paid fourteen euros for. Later that week I discover some items missing that were supposed to be handy for camping. Thank you customs, I hope you enjoyed my stuff. I begin to wonder if we had that delay because it was *my* bag that needed to be rechecked.

At the break of dawn, it's already warm outside the airport of the capital San José. Tropical smells fill the air and boy does that feel good – it smells like freedom to me!

As usual I didn't book any hotel nor did I research where I should go. As a matter of fact I didn't make any plans at all, I'm just here now. My backpack offers some Dutch baguettes with cheese for an early breakfast. Not realizing that it would be the last decent cheese for the year to come I unwittingly swallow the last bite.

Taxi drivers gather around like a pack of wolves trying to push overpriced rides. It shouldn't come as a surprise as things like that always have a counterproductive effect on me. Even though I can barely stand as I skipped a full night of sleep, not to mention my battle against the wrecking time difference, I decide to follow my instinct and brush them off, as politely as possible.

Approaching a girl with long blond hair standing by herself I ask if she is interested to share a cab to the center so we can split the costs. Enthusiastically she tells me that she is waiting for her pick-up ride from an animal rescue center where she'll be volunteering for a few weeks. Suddenly I get overtaken, yet not by unshaven revolver-swinging *banditos,* but by a *what the heck* moment. You've guessed it, that is where I end up too.

This animal rescue center (ARC) is located near the not too big of a village of San Miguel de Turrucares, basically situated in the middle of the jungle. A variety of *animales* are present, such as sloths, monkeys, macaws and owls, squirrels, dogs, pigs, goats and baby possums. You name it and it's here. Outside the cages bi-colored lizards are racing about, wild monkeys are jumping from tree to tree – enjoying their freedom. Envious looks from behind bars are thrown by other primates.

The volunteers' tasks consist of preparing food, cleaning out shit-filled cages, and maintaining the park with rakes and wheelbarrows. Close to the dorms, where boys and girls are separated by a high wall, they had a set of simple showers built, which are so cold that it is a miracle water is coming out in liquid form instead of ice cubes. One monkey, a small capuchin, has a serious condition. Whenever she smells men she gets horny, and I do mean really horny. Every time I walk up she rushes to the entrance to look me straight in the eyes while sticking out her tong, making licking gestures, hanging by the hands on wire netting. Next she opens up that black leathery monkey pussy and starts squirting! Without a doubt the most hauntingly atrocious thing I've ever seen in the animal kingdom.

For some reason the owner of the facility seems to fancy me as well. Work has to be done at their previous location where all sorts of monkeys still remain. Out of the whole gathering the old fossil picks me and asks to join her in going there to assist. As I get into the car, the driver, awkwardly enough turning out to be her husband, isn't the best of drivers – to put it mildly. Making our way on suspicious trails through the wilderness he is probably dreaming away, about slurping out coconuts or something, because he manages to get his huge four-wheel drive Chevy stuck. "I told you not to make that unnecessary move," I say while letting an obvious sigh escape.

Hours pass in the scorching midday heat while I alone dig out the stranded truck with shovel and spade, on account of the driver being wheelchair bound, incapable of performing some manual labor. The lady who invited me is pacing about making some agitated conversations on her cell phone. With sweat streaming down my face and wearing long trousers because 'Who saw this coming?' I think out loud *What a wonderful first day in this country!*

As time goes by I'm starting to have second thoughts about this chaotic organization. It has a capacity to hold sixty volunteers, which they actually reach in the summer seasons due to a surplus of liberal environmentalists and tree-hugging vegetarians. Not that there is anything wrong with that, but I'm quite shocked when I find out how much money they generate while doing the math on the calculator on my iPhone. Making investments in the park itself is something the owners aren't very fond of and the costs to keep the volunteers and animals fed is hardly ten percent of the entire income. Rescued animals that have completely recovered are kept in captivity. Empty cages mean no volunteers and no volunteers means no business.

Along with others, I lose trust in the whole thing and pack my bags to leave. When an employee starts demanding to pay for a day that I wasn't even there the scheme is complete and my presumptions are confirmed. I also find out the owners of this supposed non-profit are engaged in real estate too. Momentarily they have three houses on the market, I mean nice ones. With outdoor pools and stuff. Too bad they exploit their country's situation to roll the dice. So much for *Pura Vida* (meaning Pure Life, a Costa Rican saying).

Eager for some excitement, a handful of other backpackers and I rent an affordable van to head to the Arenal volcano together, commonly known as an area with mostly flat land. Wild macaws fill the airspace and if you're favored as I am you can spot toucans. We also visit the hidden-away waterfall of *Rio Fortuna*, obscured in green.

It is here where large hills aren't shy anymore to show themselves. A true oasis unfolds with a stretched waterfall that crashes into this turquoise lagoon. Also it's full of those typical jungle trees with long lianas and big bright leaves that hang like natural umbrellas from the cliffs. The cartoon of *Jungle Book* from my childhood is coming alive!

Once used to the cold water we spend some time swimming, me in my boxers because I forgot my swimming shorts, but I don't care. Close to the village of La Fortuna the day of semi-planned activities ends by chilling in the natural hot springs. The underlying masses of lava, streams into the upper layers of the earth which makes the water of the springs really hot, so we are being nearly boiled alive like lobsters in a pan. With something as special as this you have to bear in mind that it's somewhat touristic out here. When the group intends to return to the San José area in our rented van I split from them to go my own way. It's about time for some old-fashioned action, the open road calling my name, it beckons me to follow the unknown path.

Fully equipped, I dive right in by walking six kilometers in the burning sun through the greenest of green. Still on the move, a blanket of dark clouds comes rolling in from behind. Via a big traffic sign that reads La Fortuna I learn that I made it to the medium-size town itself. Literally five minutes after I check in at a random hostel a thunderstorm brews like only a monsoon can.

Torrential rain and strong winds attack all night. Speaking about strong winds, food from the ARC granted me nasty stomach cramps. Traveling overseas means you better do it with medication that knows how to treat diarrhea. I end up cynically thinking that they probably want to poison the volunteers thus preventing them from getting exposed, and in order to keep new ones coming in.

To my amazement the morning heat erased all evidence of the fallen rain. That should give you an idea of how intense it already is. Several tours for the great outdoors are shuffled down my throat at the reception desk of the hostel, one of which is a canopy tour. That certainly is something that sounds like music to my ears and as a former outdoor sports instructor my heart starts beating like a German techno track from the nineties. Having signed up I'm the only participant. No wonder, the rest of the hostel is completely empty.

When an air-conditioned van drops me off on location I couldn't care less about the crocodiles in the resort pond. What interests me more are the howler monkeys in the trees making that eerie sound. High up in the green there are even sloths, I'm rejoiced to see them having a good time in the wild where they belong. Starting my tour there I go, hurling through the treetops on five-hundred-meter zip lines! What a luxury to have all five instructors to myself, all being males in their early twenties wearing tight t-shirts, and speaking English with a Spanish accent, it's like I'm trapped in a gay man's dream. As it's out of season they complain about the boredom and bad payments. Surely they squeeze a tidbit of compassion out of me, but like I really care at this moment, I have other things to worry about, such as flying through the volcanic jungle at an irresponsible velocity and even more so at scary heights, but I am having the time of my life!

At the end of the parcours their latest attraction is making the hairs in the back of my neck stand up. Only a few days in use I urge them to first show and convince me it is safe, their so-called *Tarzan Swing,* for I do not have a death wish whatsoever. Scoping the scene, the *Tarzan Swing* is as follows, you basically jump off a platform from about seventy-six meters off the ground, obviously attached to a cord but it's still harrowing. There is a significant free fall before the cord starts carrying your weight and you actually start swinging. As the first foreign tourist to try it out I suggest that one has to have some balls jumping down towards a certain death. As I go I chant as loud as I can, "I can see my house from here!" echoing through the small valley. The instructors laugh. Overwhelmed by euphoria I keep swinging back and forth down below thinking to myself *Let's do this again!* Although zip lines at the famous location of *Monteverde Extremo* are longer and the swing slightly higher, this one is just as much fun. At least here you don't have to stand in line and wait your turn.

Going back to the village in the same van I am surprised by its transformation. In mere hours the whole village changed into a place with banners and flags with the national colors red, white and blue. I find stands with salivating smells of grilled meat, loud music everywhere, interrupted by a brass band marching through the street. Everyone is wearing their best outfit and seems thrilled as it turns out to be Independence Day over here. Lovely people in a beautiful area with plenty of activities – this is a town to spend a few days in.

Costa Rica, used as a set of many epic blockbuster movies, is a slenderized country crammed inbetween the Caribbean Sea on the east and the Pacific Ocean on the west, with a mountain range in the middle. With a relatively small acreage it is rare to have certain parts boasting different climates. For instance, in the center it is raining almost non-stop whereas temperatures on both coasts happen to be quite satisfying in the raining season, which it is now.

Public transportation takes me to a marvelous place in south-central, where I soon come in contact with sun-tanned residents, getting ready for the high season. They actually came up with a synonym for the busy months ahead that will undoubtedly speak to anyone's imagination, i.e. 'Gringolandia'. Even though it is a racially discriminatory term referring to white tourists, I don't think anyone will really be offended by being compared to someone from Victorian times owning land and people – assuming that this time everyone will get along. At small local markets I'm happy to indulge in life-size avocados, my favorite piece of fruit, which is often mistaken for an ordinary vegetable. It grows all across the country so it is heaven for me, since you won't taste better ones anywhere else.

Between three and five in the afternoon thunder starts with spectacular flashes and unstoppable rains, and the next day the shower repeats itself. The inhabitants generally like it easy going. It's one of the few countries that doesn't even have an army! Of course, befriended Uncle Sam keeps an eye on the place. It's quite expensive however, as the only thinkable downside, maybe for the same reason just mentioned. Many travelers refer to it as the 'Switzerland of Central America'. Air-conditioned interstate tour buses going all over are somewhat modestly priced. A ride in one of those gets me to Punta Arenas via the town of San Ramón. Except for fresh fish dinners in cozy restaurants on the ocean view boulevard, there is not much to do. Run-down buildings and impoverished neighborhoods are kind of dirty, so unless you have some specific goal you don't want to stay here for too long. Having to use public transport all the time makes me think of getting my own vehicle but it's relatively expensive so I promise myself to buy me a motorcycle in the next country I will visit. I already can't wait.

As there are few options left for now I am back at it again the next day, slouching in my bus seat, eventually leading me right outside of the city of Quepos where I check in at a youth hostel. From here the energetic village of Manuel Antonio is only about a ten-minute drive, famous for its homonymous national park as well as surfing beaches, perfect for beginners and advanced alike. Some Western enthusiasts brought along their own board, but for a trifle you can rent one at a stall on the beach for some hours or even the whole day. Lessons are affordable and sometimes free, especially for girls. My youth hostel offers a swimming pool and multiple hammocks from where you can see the sun set in the ocean. Need I say more? My face and shoulders are sunburnt and the sensitiveness will only get worse in the next couple of days. I absolutely love it.

On my way coming here I met a young Dutch traveler who has an amusing spirit, and at the same time seems chronically annoyed about everything, especially the prices. He is also very impatient and right away I recognize myself in him from when I was younger. It feels like I time-travelled into the future and get to see how useless all those worries were. It is nothing short of confrontational and funny to me in its own weird way.

When I visit the national park with my so-called younger self we are disappointed by all the empty promises given. Yes, the white sand beaches are astoundingly gorgeous, and exotic looking palm trees satisfy the needs for flora, but wildlife aka fauna, seems nonexistent and that's the reason we came here for. In fact, we see more monkeys once we exit the overpriced park, mostly capuchin. Others claim that we are unlucky today when they show us pictures on their cameras of all sorts of beasts. Sometimes you have to have some luck too.

Shortly after, that is exactly what I find: some luck. With more guys and girls from the hostel to join us we visit a paradisiacal strip of beach. Shallow waters are of pleasant temperature. Our interest is sparked by people offering trips for parasailing. You know, more or less hanging behind a speedboat attached to a parachute. Of course it's way too expensive according to my younger self, who rejects even considering to pay for this intrepid getaway. As if it's written in the stars, a Mexican homosexual invites me to take a chance without having to pay for anything. At the time of the offer, I did not yet know that he was attracted to the same sex. Once airborne I start having assumptions due to his advances for a little bit of intimacy. Careless as I am I start singing "Love is in the air", just for fun. Looking straight into his eyes I promise him I am as straight as a cannon barrel on a Navy ship. On second thought, bringing up the uniformed sailors probably only gets him more in the mood. Either way I think I made it clear I am more on the traditional side of things. Long story short, to partake in the experience where you can feel what a bird must feel like, is really cool. As you ascend, it is noticeable how quickly sounds disappear such as the rolling of billows below. I'm sure parasailing is nice at the Spanish Costa Brava, still, by no means it can top the view on green overgrown islands and dense jungles. Of course, what makes it all the more special is being so far away from home. Somehow giving it a bit of a different dimension. At least that is the effect it has on me. Landing in the warm water I coincidentally get to kill two birds with one stone as we climb on a jet ski to bring us back ashore. Never did that before either. If you could only see the look on my younger self's face, who is still flabbergasted about how it's given to revel in all these costly things without recompense. Consider it a lesson in Karma, for if you are a generous person and not acting stingy, things will truly come your way.

Ending up in these break loose things only ripen life and it was all for free. It won't likely come your way if you are just sitting at home waiting for that redeeming miracle to happen, enviously staring at brainless celebrities on gameshows on TV doing all that cool stuff you could do yourself. It's almost like that old story where a bunch of dudes get coins from their master, I'm sure you have heard it before somewhere. The one that buried his share in fear of loosing it gets nothing in the end while the one that invested his coins prospers and gets even more. That's the way it goes.

Ultimate freedom involves taking risk, and believe me, a certain someone who raised me that I was heavily influenced by, bless her heart, is more like the first one. Even if it takes serious effort to break free from that mindset, once you've overcome, it will pay off.

On the last night of her stay I am holding hands with a Canadian black girl. Trudeau would be so proud in support of the diversity agenda. Though this time it serves a purpose. As if a Canadian person of color isn't random enough, as opposed to the stereotypical lumberjacks in red and black hankered shirts, this cutie decided to get another piercing in one of her ears. In the back of an unhygienic tattoo parlor down a dark suspicious ally she's ordered to lie on the stretcher. Her firm grip gives away that it must be painful when the pin pushes away cartilage.

The funny thing is that I met this girl about thirty minutes ago while buying juice at a timber kiosk in the streets. She impulsively invited me to tag along and I said yes and just like that we shared an intense moment together that can only occur if you put yourself open to volatility. Immediately parting ways after the act due to her schedule, we never see or talk to each other again, making me realize that these things, connecting with another human being like that, are priceless.

That evening more priceless things are in sight as I'm attending a barbecue in Quepos in an Airbnb with new friends that I previously met in the ARC. A peculiar case arises when we find out that a funny man from South Africa knows a friend of mine from the Netherlands, having met a few months ago in Asia, proving the world is small for folks roaming it.

The good memories however, begin with a hazel-skinned lady, who demonstrates in her own romantic way that she's more than interested in me. It is hard to withstand the looks of this natural beauty. Well, at least now she is, one successful nose job later. Her abundant liquor intake is probably to blame for somehow making her snobbish London attitude seem sexy. Vowing to see her again she's still in dreamland when I silently exit the double bed and quietly leave the apartment with the first rays of sunshine.

In contrast to the country's general fairness, the taxi drivers are scamming tourists on a large scale. In short rides as well as the longer ones they charge double the amount without moving a muscle, not realizing they are biting the hand that feeds them. Wherever you go try to take one of the plentiful available buses that come in all sorts and sizes. The one I'm having today is rugged, ugly and far from spacious for my European legs. Nonetheless, I get what I pay for when it brings me from point A to B. Personally I think it's very enjoyable to be the only white guy in most, if not all, buses I take. Sitting among people from the country I get to really soak in the culture, all the while we are passing a lot of green where it's not uncommon to bump into wild tapirs, the ant-eating creatures.

Down the route I'm not leaving the Elysian hills of a small town named Dominical before sliding off of a seven meters high waterfall, before continuing the way to the coastal village of laid-back Uvita, another one of those places where the warm breeze makes the tall palm trees, that are densely and abundantly distributed, doing the waltz together, draped in sunshine. Here I need to be for some once-in-a-lifetime sightseeing.

Cellophane foil still embraces my arm from Jaco Beach, which is pronounced as 'hakko beach', where I got a new tattoo at *Anchor's end*. The artist kept complimenting me saying that this is the coolest piece he's ever made. You know you are good with needles if your client falls asleep while tattooing him, as I had that happening to me, being all rosy from the exposure of surfing in the blistering heat too long. According to myth, the inside of your arm is supposed to be one of the most sensitive parts of your body, yet I still found a way to fall asleep on a simple stretcher.

Over at the bay this completely 'cast away' type of beach belt is very scenic whereas over at my hostel not so much. Here one incident gets so crazy that I needed to call the guard at night for assistance. As I am staying in a dormitory, my drunken roommates are continually cursing hippies who are blasting horrible music out of a sound system that makes one wonder why anyone would travel with a thing that size in the first place. That's not very considerate at all while sharing a room with others. Pissing with an open bathroom door is already close to the limit, but when they start smoking pot in the room when I'm about to go to sleep, I snap. Apart from it being against the house rules I care not what folks put into their own bodies, just don't hassle me with it. Or am I being unreasonable here? Luckily the big night guard makes sure I never see them again, and I have a wonderful quiet night after all, having the room to myself now. Leaning on the window sill with the window open, watching the gob-slobbers leave I call after them, *"Sayonara pendejos!"*

In the morning the owner of the establishment apologizes with the invitation to join him and his English teacher for lunch. More as a way to make up for the inconvenience. I've always preferred giving to people instead of receiving from them, though throughout the years I have learned that turning down free food will only take away its blessing. Therefore, the three of us find ourselves at the edge of town where no man has gone before. Quite literally too I might add, because his English teacher is a lady, he himself is a raging

25

homosexual with unconstrained feminine traits, and I am, well, the first real and only man at the scene I suppose! They serve a local dish, a bowl of rice with chunks of chicken, and a soup so rich in veggies that I cannot walk anymore after eating. That sure balances things out.

So as I was saying, I need to be in Uvita for the next once-in-a-lifetime sightseeing opportunity. According to travel guidebooks of fellow travelers this is the place to be if one desires to spot dolphins and whales and that is the exact reason we are here. I say *we* because I hooked up with the girl I met at the airport on my first day, who by the way happens to be Dutch as well. Me being nearly twice her age and from a totally different generation is not an issue. No matter what your background is or where you're coming from, striving towards the same goal unites people, and that goal is being organic with the nature around and freeing yourself from the systematic bondages all of us are born into. That is the fundamental beauty of backpacking.

Boarding the boat with a capacity to hold a dozen people makes me seasick as heck pretty much right away. As I am getting ready to throw up any moment now, I can't help to think that my medication for motion sickness is a mockery to your face. Preliminary hanging half across the rail my view spins and turns as well as my stomach. I'm tempted to say that for once it's worth the agony. How often do you get to see dolphins swimming along? Not showing any sign of fear they playfully jump out of the ocean, the water having a majestic deep blue color and its temperature is slightly cooler than expected. The boat cuts the engine to let the fish species draw near, soon after, multiple whales cruise at a distance of thirty meters from where we sit.

It's an absolute highlight of my trip thus far, as they so classically blow air and water through their blowholes behind their heads, making that unprecedented sound that I only know from documentary films. Looking at the gigantic animals it makes you think about what else is down there below the surface, deep into the ocean's ravines? An interesting observation, however, is that from all the people on board I am the only one who sees the whales with his own eyes. Others watch them through the little screen of their cell phones and digital cameras. My footage may be of lesser quality; the memory will forever be projected on my retina, it is good to be in the moment sometimes. While getting out of the boat back at the beach, I am more than aware where I place my foot, for we were warned that it's stingray infested. And what do you know? It doesn't take very long for us to spot one.

On my way to the next startling discovery, I am back on one of those infamous torn-up buses. Crimson chairs resemble benches in the puffy shape of those traditional American diner booths. These buses could easily be from the sixties, if not a decade older. All this time the horrible rain from last night hasn't stopped.

I am dressed in sneakers without socks wearing my swimming shorts, and a blue raincoat. It looks ridiculous but in any case it does the trick.

Going deeper into a remote region the bus passes a village called Paracito. Invisible hands tear the slab of grey clouds wide open, revealing patches of blue, turning edges of the pressing slab bright. Through the moist-coated window, I see groups of vultures in the dead trees drying their wings in the liberating heat of the sun.

Away from civilization I am heading towards the region of Palmar Sur, de Osa Puntarenas, clearly the road less travelled. Wooden houses in variable sizes are built on wooden poles at the border of the outback. The once so bright colors losing the battle against the elements, layers of paint slowly flaking off. All of them are rotting away due to bad maintenance, or rather the absence thereof, how characteristic. Without a doubt the most beautiful area from what I have seen. It feels as if I'm lost in the unending forests of the Amazonia or something. All there is are miles and miles of palm trees, banana plantains, plant nurseries for God-knows-what and green bushes too dense to see through.

Switching buses a few times, guessing I choose the right ones, the day is half spent when I arrive at the mystical place of a long-held dream. Although I asked the bus driver upfront to signal me when to get out, my eyes are on eagle mode and I already see the sign from afar, with my daypack already in my hand. A white sign with black letters reads *Finca 6,* my destination.

I almost can't believe I am really here, after so many years of diligent research and obsession, at the not so well known placement of *Las Bolas.* Throughout this land are hundreds of stone spheres scattered about, for miles apart, shrouded in mystery.

The official story is that they were used in ceremonies and rituals, the unofficial story is that they haven't got a clue, and my personal findings have led me to believe, when they were still on their original location, they represented star constellations.

Seeing them in the middle of the jungle is a visual climax for me. To touch them, measure them, smell them, study them, they have fascinated me for years. Not many people know about the hybrid statues that have been found here as well, confirming the scrolls of oral literature having withstood throughout the ages. Today hidden from the public to eradicate even the smallest piece of evidence of antiquities we're not supposed to know of.

Right here and now I receive that I made the right choice giving up the social security I had in the Netherlands. Putting all my belongings in a storage, giving up my cozy farm on the countryside, putting my company on hold with the risk of losing it, and choosing, at least for now, a life filled with insecurities. This is one of those moments where I understand when people back home tell me, "I couldn't do what you are doing, just pack and go and leave everything behind!" It brings so much joy and peace of mind being here. Squeaky bird sounds, big bright flowers, exotic butterflies cavorting about, and I get bitten by mosquitos more often than the three weeks prior to this combined. But today I'm awarded to be the only person in the beautiful park, and as in many times before, probably the only Westerner in the whole wide neighborhood. This is making those dreams reality.

Not fully saturated with the untouched forgotten surroundings I decide to start walking back, to slowly sponge it in. Even though the drizzle has turned into actual rain, I don't mind. I am dressed for the occasion. Not knowing where I'll end up, it's quite a way back to the first decent town and all this time a dog with the friendliest face is following me about.

After a while a car advances through the growing puddles. How about that, it is Maria pulling over, the woman who works at the museum at *Finca 6*. She offers shelter from the rain, and interestingly a ride into town, despite having to pass her own house for not a short distance. With disappointment in his eyes the dog watches me step into the vehicle. For being two complete strangers our following exchange of words are very open hearted. Without hindrance we speak about our lives and share personal feelings. To say without hindrance is not entirely true, mind you, all of this happens in very little English because she doesn't speak any, in very little Spanish because I don't speak any, and some French of which neither of us hardly know anything about. Our connection doesn't go unnoticed by both sides. To some extent our goodbye feels awkward because of that.

Months later and a couple of countries further south, I send a postcard to the museum addressing her by her first name, essentially that is all the information I have about her. As a way of saying thank you for her random act of kindness I suppose. A response follows quickly in my mailbox as I had left her my e-mail address. Despite the language barrier and thanks to Google Translate we develop a friendship that lasts till this day.

If I had never taken the boldness to write to her I would have never known she purposely finished work early to try to find me, for she knew there weren't any buses going all the way back into town. Where *I* am from it is considered strange to pick up hitchhikers, let alone offer rides to foreigners minding their own business walking next to the road. Now you see what beautiful things can flow forth from treating others as you would like to be treated yourself.

It is definitely one of my inherent values to treat others to the best of my knowledge, in addition, I like to keep my word, including to myself. Since I vowed to see the eyeful bird from London again, that I had left alone between the sheets in Quepos that morning, I am on the move again but this time eastward to the Caribbean coast. You have to know that I would have visited the fishers village of Puerto Viejo anyway. Having it hitherto carefully encircled on my roadmap.

The village heralds a healthy dose of sunshine, buzzing hummingbirds looking for sweets, a gentle saltwater breeze, and sympathetic people. As the sun further sets at far away horizons, the pink sky turns into dark purple while fireflies cheer up the grassy fields. Streets without lampposts are bright enough to see where you walk due to a silver gloom radiating off the crater-filled moon.

I know I am in the right place when warm water exits the showers. Now I can really wash the month old dirt from a body that only had freezing cold showers so far. Located in the only area free from touristy parts, this hostel provides space to find yourself again. The emigrated owners, a Spanish couple, cannot care less to smoke pot in front of their own guests. As soon as their kids are put to bed they are sucking joints all night, sometimes even with their own guests. Such type of liberty attracts most people that make the move.

My sexy British fling and I have a pleasant reunion. For the first night we are both fine with not sharing rooms. Unfortunately, she has been sick for days and I am on the floor of the bathroom hugging the toilet; I already had second thoughts about that suspicious chicken kebab, all night I vomit the glazing off of the porcelain. When recovery for both draws nigh some privacy is longed for.

While snooping around town, a wooden blue painted hotel

proposes itself, accompanied with healthy and fine dishes on the menu. May you ever be in the vicinity you might want to take into consideration that the ATMs are usually out of money in the weekends, and if you're unlucky in the following days as well. Depending on a simple thing as the weather, this place being somewhat hard to reach. Not to mention reasons like national holidays or local feasts and festivals, because then they are guaranteed to be hollow on the inside. Once the stock is supplemented, you will find queues of worried tourists extending to the next street corner. In worst case scenario there is the travel community which you can always rely on. Back home, people won't even grant you a dime, yet while backpacking strangers borrow each other stacks of money as if they were the best of friends for decades. Hearing stories like that or seeing it unfolding in front of my eyes, occasionally experiencing it myself, makes me very happy. Amidst the affliction there's still hope for humanity.

Strolling hand in hand through dusty streets, we bump into a pissed-off Australian girl whom we had volunteered with at the ARC. She was just rejected at the Panamanian border among other backpackers, on reason for not being able to show a flight ticket out of the country! What kind of a new rule is this? On top of that, she ended up taking a bus back that stopped every minute to pick up new waving passengers, amplifying the crankiness.

Since I am still in contact with my younger self, I send him a text message to find out if he was held up too or anything, knowing he was supposed to go in the same direction. Apparently, he crossed the border more smoothly than Grace Jones' face in the late eighties. In approximately two weeks from now, I will have to cross that border myself too. Now hearing that it is a pain in the ass for many, I find myself in a hot spot. I guess I will find out soon enough.

With the Aussie girl under our wings, she is comforted with a bunch of strong cocktails during happy hour at some beach club at night. Sharing the burden is what it is all about. In following days, we catch up while pedaling to the white shores of *Playa Punta Uva* on our rented bicycles. Empty beaches, hunched palm trees and wild pelicans. What a beauty of an untouched rainforest this eastern coastline is. Howler monkeys in the trees, crocodiles in the swamps, rodents in the jungle, and hardly anyone on the road. The glorious national park of *Refugio Nacional Gandoca-Manzanillo*, often skipped by travelers, is big enough to spend a good day in. Here you can find several types of carnivorous plants that are an amusing sight, for when you touch them with your finger the leaves snap shut, designed for capturing insects.

Not yet spoiled by old retired foreigners I am keeping my eyes open for a good piece of real estate as we cycle along. You know I would not mind building a little nest here myself either. Unfortunately, from what I have seen so far, it's big ticket property only.

When time has come for the multi national trio to split up, only the two of us take a local bus to Cahuita, not even an hour north from where we came. This little retreat is praised for its clear blue water, vegetation with the sweetest edible fruits, monkeys in the entangled mangrove, and shy toucans for lucky eyes, once again counting my own among them. A rented log cabin with a cozy porch seems like an appropriate way to spend our final days together, for my summer fling has to fly back to England. About a hundred meters from our stay lies the well-known Playa Negra, a beach with black sand as the name already gives away. Before going to bed at night, I find the terrace is a perfect spot to chill in the comfortable hammocks. I hope that the transparent geckos hanging upside down above me will stick where they are. Multitudes of small bats boldly slurp the sweetness out of a nearby plant. It is easy to imagine that Costa Rica belongs to the list of twenty countries with the largest biodiversity in the world. On the last night inside the cabin, it's sleepy time when we are surrounded with jungle sounds as well as the humming of the ventilator on the ceiling. In early November, it can be humid and boiling hot in Cahuita.

Aside from the shower head catching on fire, ignited by sparks from wires sticking out, almost killing us in the process by electrification of powered water, it has been a place of absolute tranquility.

Being on my own again in the realm of Central America, I board a white shuttle bus. Going further east through the more deteriorated parts of the country, defined by dusty streets and poorly constructed houses, a rusty sign lets me know that I have reached the border town of Sixaola. With reserved pain in my heart, I skipped the northwest to cut the costs. Guess I will not be seeing baby tortoises crawling out of their eggshells making their way towards the sea. From what others have told me I made the wrong decision by not going there, however, the south is waiting for me. Besides, I would probably need three lifetimes to see all the places worth visiting anyway. My online purchased bus ticket reads my next destination Bocas del Toro – being a group of paradisiacal party islands in the north of Panama.

Destiny however does not allow me to go there. At Border Control I'm denied access into this neighboring country. Just like so many other tourists lately, all getting rejected. What are they so scared of? We are bringing money *into* the country which would only benefit the economy.

In a later attempt to enter, I deliver a professionally fabricated flight ticket. I guess I never had a chance when uptight customs instantly recognize my face. Upon checking my flight, they discover it does not exist. Now I completely blew my chances. I have heard of tricks, people reserving plane tickets at cooperative tour operators and canceling them later. Without having available internet, I am not prepared to fix the situation now. Frankly, I was not expecting this whole charade. Neither do I have the energy to wait a few more days and try it a third time, even though that tactic has served me well in the past.

So here we walk on the bridge over the river *Rio Sixaola*, which is the border dividing the two countries. I am being escorted back by gruff soldiers in uniforms since I already exited Costa Rica. Paperwork is going so slow that I begin to believe I did see tortoises after all. Not often will you find me in a cranky mood but this is one of those moments, and just like the pissed-off Australian girl I'm having to endure that same shitty bus ride back, that stops every freaking minute to pick up everyone who stands there waving alongside the cracky tarmac. Meaning literally everyone, thus taking hours and hours to go back to Puerto Viejo in the sticky heat. A trip that could have easily been done in half the time. To bring it mildly I am not amused.

But what am I even complaining about? One month has passed and who knows how many more to go! If you don't assert yourself too flexible, you shall only find yourself in meaningless frustration. Getting disappointed at times is part of the deal, life is what happens either at home or on the road. Assess the situation, accept your circumstances, and you will be ready to change course. An essential quality to master. In this case however, the only available option left to get out of this situation does really suck.

Going all the way back to San José to take a flight becomes inevitable. And so it happens, I go back to the same city as where I arrived upon entry, where the trunks of trees along the roads are painted white. In an unforeseen moment even including being scammed by a taxi driver! His genius lie about all the bus companies having a strike that day must have worked for hundreds of other idiots, just like me.

To make matters worse, on my flight out of Costa Rica I have, ironically enough, a layover in Panama City! Equally ironic is seeing Bocas del Toro from the sky, where I was supposed to be having a great time by now, shaking my butt at pool parties with electronic music. In addition, on my connecting flight I get to see the Panama Canal as well, of which I had really hoped to cross by land, because I always admired the immense engineering project.

I can only imagine how nice it would have been to traverse this delightful green country, for from up here it looks amazing. Not providing the slightest consolation from this altitude, being so far away, but as the next best thing at least I saw its splendor. Staring out of the little airplane window, leaving the northern continent behind, I gather my strength to whisper with a soft sad voice "Hasta luego Centroamérica!"

3

COLOMBIA - SAGA UNO

Imagine if you will, to set your mind on being in one country but then ending up in another; that sure takes time of getting used to. Previously made plans can be thrown out of the window. Being rejected at the border I am more or less forced to make new plans on the spot. Do yourself a big favor by preparing your mind for a ton of uncertainties when traveling.

With Panama out of the picture beyond my power to change that, quick decision-making solves the idleness. After arriving in Colombia's capital and spending two days there, I intend to never come back. Ignorant of how that would play out later. I spend only one full day in Bogotá. Partly with the Australian girl from the ARC, who flew one day ahead of me and coincidentally stays in the same hostel.

It is amazing how much can happen in one day alone. It all starts, once I get myself some *pesos*, with spending almost two hours at a barbershop for a haircut description of "A little bit shorter please." I might not speak one word of Spanish but how hard can it be? Sitting ready in a barber cape, the agitated employees suddenly press a cellphone to my ear where I try to converse with people who claim to speak English. Some that are gathered around me are discussing my hair while others eagerly show me different hairstyles in magazines. If you know how short my hair is (being one fingertip at the time) this attempt, that is bound to fail, should be in the Guinness book of world records.

In the afternoon things get more crazy for the dress-wearing Aussie and I, as we roam traffic-filled streets, overflowing from suffocating pollution. To begin with, a local singer performing with his band from a balcony. Plenty of reporters and journalists mingle themselves among a good crowd of fans and bystanders, responsible for blocking the entire intersection. A few blocks down, a uniformed man is guarding an ATM with a gigantic double-barreled shotgun. Not a bank or something but just a money machine! That makes you wonder what event took place to turn to such drastic measures.

Furthermore, I am scammed in a chicken fast-food restaurant and if that isn't enough, a homeless guy in front of a church opposite the Bolívar Square is masturbating in broad daylight. However, it doesn't stop there. In this city of ten million people, we witness the entire police force doing absolutely nothing due to a soccer match on television. Officers neglect any kind of tumult amongst the congregated masses - all wearing yellow jerseys in support of the national team. On our way to the Monserrate mountain, of which we enjoy a citywide view from later that day, my friend is almost mugged. Apparently, you cannot ask anyone for directions these days without someone trying to stick their hands down your pocket. Don't mistake a stranger's trickery for kindness.

While strolling through the historical area of Candelaria, we are left surprised by the colorful colonial mansions in yellow-ochre and coral with the most beautiful woodcuttings made of dark mahogany. Something even more surprising is the fact we are being warned by more than five individuals to turn around. They demand for us to get the hell out of the district before ending up being killed. For ruthless gang members, born with a disregard for human life, not hesitating for a second to use violence, still don't belong to the past unfortunately. If that does not make you have second thoughts about a place, I don't know what will. All these unexpected events do not get us down though. We both crack up as the Aussie, in that typical *down under* vocabulary, says her legendary words when we see an uncommon animal at the entrance of the cable carts, that we still remind each other about regularly: "Hey look, a fucking llama!"

After those first glimpses of the country, how could I have guessed that my planned four weeks would turn into four months? Only to return at the end of my trip to spend another month. Most likely one of the best places I've ever went to. In colder areas in the evenings people are sitting in restaurants with their coats still on, and it is no exception to see suited businessmen on their way to work on a small BMX bicycle. They seem far less concerned about making a good impression by their colleagues. How about hippy-like street artists who are breakdancing in front of red traffic lights? Some even manage to juggle with three machetes! Just when I think I have seen it all, a couple of sturdy police officers drive by on tough dirt bikes, carrying little pink backpacks. Let's presume and hope they belong to their own daughters. In countrysides and downtown areas alike, grannies mooch about in worn-out tank tops without a bra. What a place to be!

A cheap airplane drops me off in the north at the Caribbean coast. As soon as I leave the airport of Cartagena, Colombia's fifth largest city, sweat starts dripping out of my pores. Blue sky, tropical bird sounds, and sunshine in abundance. This is one lively city with upbeat colors and characteristic Victorian style buildings. Founded in the fifteen hundreds it has a rich history. Contradicting that richness is the poverty that came along with it, unfortunately adding a dark touch to it. From the Castillo San Felipe, a huge fort built with light complexioned stone, you have a wonderful view of the skyline.

Interestingly enough, designed by a Dutch architect - those darn Freemasons are everywhere I tell you. Right away, I find myself addicted to the freshly prepared fruit juices, that are found everywhere throughout the narrow streets. Without a doubt, papaya and maracuya are sweeter than anywhere else. As my ultimate favorite, I order at least once a day a *limonada de coco*. This local beverage is so good that it should be served worldwide.

Since nobody wants to miss out on the fun I meet up, for one last time, with the Australian, who has also come to the city. When you backpack South America it's quite common to run in to each other now and again. Today, mostly due to social media, it's inspiring to see small travel communities come into existence everywhere I go, where backpackers let each other know where they are and search for chances to spend some time together. The center is surrounded by an impressive eleven-kilometer-long wall, mostly built by African slaves, after they were sold by other Africans.

Slurping our ice creams, we are interrupted by a very funny historian who makes his money nowadays as a tour guide. He convinces us to show us around. In the most entertaining way he teaches all the ins and outs that no history book could match up to. It seems he isn't bothered that he spent sixteen years of his life in a Miami prison. As that was the duration of the sentence he got for drug trafficking. Now finding joy in showing tourists around, his smuggling days are over. However, it takes him little effort to get two grams of cocaine when my friend asks for some good stuff.

And good it is. The absurd evening starts as we hop on the so-called 'party bus' with half-demented old folks. It basically looks like a modified school bus with open sides and an insane amount of colorful lights and loud music, as some sort of pimp wagon. For a minimal fee you can get utterly smashed as they serve alcohol while touring about town, where palm trees relish in the mild breeze. Only to later end up in a handful of dodgy clubs and bars where we dance the night away with the young and old. A certain genre of music blasting out from the huge speakers is usually detestable to my ears; a mixture between reggaeton and salsa, where the rhythm of every single song is nearly the same and the beat annoyingly monotone.

As we crash into the nightlife the next evening I get another *white mustache*. Surely, you are not that often in Colombia! Being in the place where the magical white powder pretty much originated from, you cannot withhold yourself for trying it at least once, and with once I mean a couple of grams. For starters, around here you'll get it uncut and in the purest form, and second, it is really ridiculously cheap. Scarcely dressed girls dancing on the bar are emptying bottles of rum into their own mouths, and pouring it into bystanders as if it was water. It gets pretty wild. Holding the bottles continuously upside down the floor gets flooded with gallons of alcoholic drinks. We party until our clothes get sticky and our new bags of cocaine are finished also. I am completely new to this drug, but according to some regular users, this is the best stuff they have ever tried. Needing a few days to get my act together I take their word for it.

I think we can all agree it's a sad reality that many tourists solely come for the drugs. It is not as if you have to search for it or anything, since it's being offered on every street corner wherever you go. It is disturbing and frankly quite shocking how much marihuana and cocaine is being consumed by both tourists and locals alike, at least in the area's I visit. Excessive drug use is not the only disturbing thing. I did not want to bring it up so soon because these lands have so much richness to bestow upon, but let's get it over with.

Another major attraction are the *mujeres*, the women. Particularly speaking prostitutes. They are everywhere and they are many. Some way too young. With ultimate feminine features of slim waistline and round curves their beauty is unparalleled. Turning the focus on the general public for a moment it has to be said that a lot of cheating and unfaithfulness is going on. In all these months, I hardly meet anyone who isn't divorced or only married once. On larger scale, the sex industry is a huge income for the country. On smaller scale, it is a mediocre income for the girls who support themselves and their children because more often than not are they single mothers, of which an epidemic is going on.

A lot of girls do it out of necessity, using their earnings to support the household including mom, dad, or even grandparents. It might be easy for us to judge them from our comfortable seats. I am not ashamed to say that I have great respect for some of them doing this kind of work, sacrificing themselves for the sake of helping others. Before researching this topic I might have previously stated that there is always a way to earn money, after facing the facts however, sometimes there just aren't other means.

That having said, the majority of women have a general interest in foreigners, not shying away from letting you know if they are interested. I did not think I would still be in the front seats of the market with my age but boy what a boost! Maybe my bright blue eyes are to blame for the women shamelessly calling after me in the streets - flirting, hissing, catcalling, everything! Even when I walk together with a female backpacker, that easily could have been my spouse for all they care, they call after me as if they need to have their primordial lusts satisfied on the spot. They even approach me in the supermarket asking for my phone number.

On account of wanting to see the country itself, I don't waste my time getting into the many requests. But of course, I'm not a saint either. On one of these eye-meeting occurrences, I meet a lovely lady who is pretty straight forward. Having had a drink or two in the evening, I experience the passion of Colombian women. Since it is common here to live together with the whole family we are bound to finding a hotel room. After taking off my trousers she observes me from head to toe before mentioning her surprise that I am not black.

Best compliment ever. As if I hadn't noticed already, she goes on to explain how casual meetings are part of Colombian culture. In a turn of events, that statement would prove itself true once again, albeit much sooner than expected.

Walking back to my hostel in the early hours, still with an afterglow of what just happened, I realize she couldn't have made a more compelling point. Going through narrow streets of the artistic neighborhood of Getsemani, filled with smoke of nightly street barbecues, I bump into a gorgeous girl with eyes that captivate me straight away. The tinted angel wears a white dress with glowing long black hair, covering her whole back like a sateen veil. I don't speak Spanish and she hasn't even heard of the word English, but it turns out we both speak the language of love, as corny as that may sound. After a lukewarm shower, I gather all my strength to go again and we make sensuous love for the remainder of the night. When finally going to sleep in the morning I think to myself (as any bachelor would) *If this is a precursor for the rest of my stay I am going to have the time of my life!*

Barranquilla is known for its extravagant Carnaval. At the appointed time, the somewhat dull city, also on the northern coast, turns into a playful battlefield, where nine months later babies are being born. Because it's not that time of year I skip it for now as I am taking the bus eastward. I figuratively set sail to an unpopular small strip of beach. Playa del Ritmo is good for relaxing in hammocks and kayaking along blue shallow waters of the undeveloped coastline, where sand and rocks intersperse. Whereas the last pursuit is almost my last one in life, when humidity concludes to throw in sudden thunder and lightning while being in open water. Thank God, I make it out in time before turning into a *humano a la plancha*. Safely ashore, a glass jar of the sweetest fresh maracuya juice settles the deal.

Together with a bearded German, I share a taxi to a large nearby city. Santa Marta is known for housing the oldest cathedral of South

America, with a fitting name the *Cathedral de Santa Marta,* as well as the oldest house of the entire continent, *La Casa de la Aduana.* Remarkable isn't it? The first house ever built and it's the Customs; just what we need. Although I get the idea that it is relatively safe, hearing the story of a befriended backpacker, coincidentally being in the vicinity as well, brings me to rethink previous conclusions. Namely she gets robbed of her valuables by two guys holding guns to her head in her very hotel! I can think of nicer ways to wake up. Meeting more travelers, plenty of stories circle around about individuals having all their belongings stolen. Cellphones, passports, money, entire backpacks, etcetera. Almost everyone knows someone that has been mugged in one way or another. One of the few downsides of this place, but what do you expect? Only half a decade ago Colombia was considered the most dangerous country in the world. Now on the rise and I predict that in the next ten years it will become one of the most popular holiday destinations.

At the edge of town, there is a rough district where the Red Cross is active on a daily basis. Being outright dangerous, you should avoid going there. Having blend between the locals, a crappy minivan takes me straight through it, to end up on the other side of the hill, that is polluted with plastics. My spirits are instantly lifted when entering the small bay called Taganga. Building new homes is officially illegal here but everyone does it anyway. The hostel where I'm staying is an old luxurious mansion that belonged to some big shot from the Escobar regime. Through corruption, he actually got out of jail and every month he stops by to collect the rent, as most banking is done in cash.

Many online travel guides unrightfully denigrate this community-like village and its locals. Slandered and dragged through the virtual mud by unexperienced naive foreign students who expected all-inclusive resorts and boulevards full of clubs to get drunk. In other words, kids who are incapable of entertaining themselves and don't appreciate the natural wonders of this world. I end up spending three weeks here and love it. The only demerit is getting blisters all over my hands and pain in my lower back. I took it upon myself to help out some workmen fortifying a short cut to the beach. While lifting huge concrete pillars a path slowly forms on top of the sharp rocks. As a way of contributing to the nation's rebuilding I definitely payed my dues. I eat fresh fish on a daily basis for very acceptable prices, plenty of tasty fruits, they serve tea from fresh moringa leaves, and you will find a variety of restaurants with some of the best food around and overall I am surrounded by happy people. Sure, there are some minor details, if you can't handle a good power cut or no wifi signal then it's not your place. Moreover, local alcohol consumption borders on abuse and you get offered cocaine once or twice in the streets as a tourist, which is no different from other places. Shaped like a horseshoe the beach is not the cleanest and the absence of brick streets causes dirt when it rains, but so what? Diving courses are among the cheapest in the world and hostels also have swimming pools. For those who like music; huge speakers belonging to stores and beach bars fan out energizing melodies all day. Chilling on sun-lit rooftops, you get to read a book or share thoughts with others while sipping refreshing cocktails. What's not to like?

It is also an ideal base to plan tours to sites and cultural hotspots. The trip to the Lost City is one such example. Going to the long-abandoned overgrown temples in the jungle is a killer activity for the outdoorsy types, which requires a good hike. Or how about visiting the nearby village of romantic Minca? Cute colorful taverns, the biggest hammock in the world and farms where you can stay for free in exchange of some not burdensome volunteer work. Right outside of it, the beauty perdures with inspiring waterfalls, shyly hiding behind the density of lush greenery and thick bundles of high-reaching bamboo, where the stream goes downward through naturally eroded stairways. Hills turn into mountains with lots of climbable jungle trails leading through banana plantains, such as the one leading towards *Los Piños*. It is named like that due to the handful of beautiful pine trees on the summit, disclosing an amazing wide view across the entire valley and the Caribbean Sea. Not too long ago, some of the mountains belonged to the FARC, who by the way are still very active in some areas. So, don't say I didn't warn you when you find yourself standing between coca plantains covering green slopes in whole. Surely, it is something I had never seen before. Something else you can stumble upon, as I find out after having walked there for a few days, are wild pumas and jaguars. Gee, thanks for the heads up!

Being in and around Santa Marta is extra special to me. It's here in the very north where the ride of a lifetime begins. My adventure of independence. Making reality of a dream I envisioned for over a decade already. Not without the necessary setbacks and effort of course. For one, trying to enter the City Hall, where women dressed in hot pants walk in, I am refused because I am wearing shorts. So, twenty-four hours later I give it another try in the burning heat of the day, wearing long trousers. At the Traffic Center, I give the required fingerprints, but I have to make up a blood type because their type of classifications are unknown to me. God let us hope I never get an accident where I need to be given blood, for assuredly they will pump the wrong blood cells through my veins with all that entails. Furthermore, I head to the notary to get legal documents signed, then repeatedly back to the store for other necessary papers, where I find out that my information isn't stored in the computers of the Traffic Center due to a malfunctioning. Thus, heading back there to start from the beginning, combined with multiple mandatory visits to the City Hall, and all without any of them speaking English. Does this sound like a holiday to you? I can't stress enough how much a holiday differs from real traveling.

Weeks go by until finally, when insurance is settled and all papers are legitimate, I drive away on my brand new motorcycle! I bought an

AKT Enduro TTR, a black cool-looking dirt bike from a Colombian brand. They import parts from China and Taiwan and assemble them in Colombian factories. So, I sort of hold true to the promise that I would never buy a Chinese motorcycle again, of which you could read in *Breaking Free*, the first part of this series of *Good to Go*. Among driving gear that I gather in the next couple of days is a helmet of the brand *Spark*. It is very exciting to see the big white letters covering both sides of my black racing helmet. Making it feel as if this is preordained, for it means 'Vonk' in Dutch, which happens to be my last name.

With six gears, it takes little time to reach Palomino, yet another coastal village. One hundred and forty kilometers per hour is fast enough in just a T-shirt and no protection. Especially with wet serpentine roads. Tall cliffs are overgrown with wild vegetation. Everything seems to be so very alive, the view from here on the piercing blue waters below is a treat to the eye. Birds of prey above are circling on the warm layers of wind. The white clothed indigenous people are animating to the soul. From the second I spot them I sense I am intrigued beyond measure. Their dark skin, odd looking hats with long black hair sticking out beneath them makes history come to life.

Straight away upon arrival, I notice this town is excessively touristic for my taste. Am I too honest when saying the strip of beach is absolutely hideous? My first impression is seldom wrong. Adding to that, a bastard doesn't appreciate my presence. My encounter with this dirty ferocious beast leaves some nasty bite marks in both hands. One of its fangs goes straight through my thumb and it hurts like hell! I am aware of setting a bad example here but I couldn't be bothered going to the doctor to get a rabies shot. I don't learn much from it though, an hour later in another spot I already have a puppy on my lap, who finds pleasure in biting in both my hands, yet this time in a playful manner. I'm a sucker for animals. Bandages are total rubbish, best described as transparent adhesive tape with some flimsy gauze. In spite of the wrapper claiming they are waterproof, coming off in a matter of minutes undeniably debuts their bold lie.

A funny thing is that everyone wears fake Crocs. You know, those rubber clogs. They come in every color imaginable. A less funny thing is the number of hostels on the way towards the beach, and more being built as we speak. My natural tendency is to shun away from tourism so I end up staying at an indigenous family. Top shelf adventure goes hand in hand with less comfort, I find out once more as the bathroom is forty yards further down a trail, and without having a lock. Showers are not even here and my bed consists of stacked pallets. The roof of my cabin however is skilfully made with interlaced palm leaves and certainly does the trick. Aside from getting hammered and continuously being high most tourists rent a big inner tube to float down the river, that comes from the mountains going straight through the village. Locals driving upstream carry the westerners on the back of their two stroke mopeds and small engine motorbikes.

During a random hike uphill through the rainforest, I watch young backpackers for a while as they scream and float by, due to the current. Deeper into the area I am accompanied by howler monkeys, tropical fruits, macaws, huge butterflies and insects that probably haven't been discovered yet. Not surprisingly I see snakes and scorpions also. Another location has a yellow one-engine airplane flying directly overhead at twelve feet. Facades of the mountains can obstruct any sound, even when it's very close. Coming out of absolutely nowhere, it almost makes me shit my pants. Having a rest at an open spot, I'm leaning with my back against a thick tree. Here too, children from one of those indigenous tribes pass frequently. I figure those huts in the distance might very well be the place they congregate. Dreaming away, I try to remember all the highlights from past months. After all, writing this book started out as a form of therapy, trying to give the experiences a place. The origins of a memoir, if you will.

Another thing sought after by the rucksack-wearing masses is the much-visited Tyrona Park. Having had a short drive west, I arrive at the same time as two fully packed touring cars. While opening their doors more jam-packed vehicles are backing up into the driveway. Hundreds of tourists block the entrance wearing Nike sport shoes and sunglasses with plate-glass, about to invade the sacred territory of the indigenous people who live here. No wonder they close off the Park for months from time to time. Luckily, I know with help from insiders there is a trail towards the beach only a mile away. Same amount of wildlife, if not more, same ocean view, just as breathtaking and completely free! It's granted to be there without the European and north American flocks. Except for having to jump aside for an iguana that shits half his bodyweight out from off a tree branch, things run calmly and peaceful.

If you have some spare time and deserts have your interest, the area of *La Guajira* is not the worst place to be. Due to hurricanes, it can only be reached by boat at this time. Therefore, I am skipping it. Instead the navigation on my new Samsung phone is guiding me south in a straight line on my roadmap. My other phone is broken since I accidentally dropped it. Thanks to the black market in Santa Marta I've got myself a new one for a very affordable price. Now it is secured between the clamps of a selfie stick that I tied to my handle bar, you have to be inventive. The progression of wandering presents birds of prey I've never seen before. Soaring by they aren't hindered by the infrastructural projects stretching miles and miles. I am being held up on the road by incredibly slow driving machines that I also have not seen before. *What are they even using those things for?* I wonder. Workmen climb on top of the vehicles which are easily as big as a house. Cutting branches off trees make it possible for them to move on, albeit slowly.

Hundreds of cars and scores of motorcycles are right behind the yellow machines, yet non of us finds a way to pass. Meanwhile dry landscapes remind me of India and wavy heathlands remind me of the Netherlands. Even on the other side of the world some areas have such a strong resemblance. Leaving the Caribbean coast of Magdalena behind I know I will not be seeing it again anytime soon. It makes me sad and excited at the same time. Pretty much the entire route the trees on either side are making a distinguished bending inward. Leaning towards each other it is like driving through a green tunnel.

Somewhere in the afternoon I enter into the city of Valledupar; it is referred to as the *green city* because of the many trees throughout. Undoubtedly, the main reason for people to have heard of this place, is due to Vallenato. This accordion-based music style has its origins here. A great favorite in all of the country, but on a personal level, to be frank, it annoys the heck out of me. Not that it is bad per se, it is just that every song is identical and it is played on the radio all day long.

After I recover from a painful ear infection, a sore throat and a serious cold with fever that floors me for two weeks, I explore the perimeter on foot. During grocery shopping at *exitó* supermarket around the corner from my hostel, people like to talk to me. Differencing from young to old, everyone approaches, and everyone watches. At another store two sixteen-year-old girls, with smiles from ear to ear, stand closer than is comfortable or should be allowed. In general, people are very friendly and interested; it feels nice that they are all so welcoming. Such a different environment from other countries I have been to. For a motorcycle check-up at a garage the ladies behind the reception desk even get up from their chairs and hug and kiss me goodbye as I go, as if we know each other for years, instead of the ten minutes in reality. It is crazy how easy it is to make contact. Since the border is close, there are many illegal girls from Venezuela. Meeting up with them delivers the next two insane stories, I like to share.

49

Even if you never follow the news you might know the political situation in Venezuela. At the time I am in the area I can easily state that the situation is worse than ever. The implemented socialism has totally wrecked the place and torn the civilization to pieces. A failed system that is responsible for millions of deaths throughout the ages, but here they thought *Why not give it one more try?* Its people don't think about what to feed the dogs, they literally eat the dogs themselves in order to stay alive. Some assure me that if I go as a white person it is the last country I will ever see. Judging from images the internet shows, things you don't get to see on the news, they could be right. In all hopelessness and desperation, many of these girls have crossed the border to escape the madness and have now turned to prostitution to survive. You don't need a trained eye to spot them as they go about their business in the streets. Me being kindhearted and compassionate towards minorities in general, almost cursed with a deep interest for anything uncommon, it doesn't take very long for me to befriend some of them.

Before I know it, I am chilling with a group of ten girls in an illegal whorehouse. Everyone dressed up in black lingerie with lace, and with their make-up on because they are waiting for a client to arrive. I have no idea how people even know that it is here on this location. When mister client does arrive, the look on his face is priceless, as he is just as surprised as I was when I callously crossed the threshold into this remarkable formula. This is the catch - besides ten gorgeous girls all in their early twenties, perfectly lined up by now for him to choose from, there is also the pimp, his fourteen-year-old brother, his cousin of six, his grandmother, and a two-month-old baby of which I know nothing about how it got there. The client finds out he has not been texting with the girl he thought he was texting with, but with the pimp instead! He did not count on this! As soon as the transaction is done the client, and one of the sculptured girls with huge fake boobs, are off to a pre-arranged hotel.

It is shocking to find out later, when I'm taken in tow, how well organized these so-called hotels are. They are solely built for the sex industry. Rooms go by the hour, taxis are driving off and on. To avoid being seen by anyone, keeping the act discrete, the walls have a little built-in hatch where the client can drop his cash. Someone really thought this through. Next, cleaning ladies work day and night to clean up after the mess, in the rooms that are supplied with condoms, wall wide mirrors and a stripper pole. This is the big money for whoever owns these kind of facilities.

A few days later, the girls show me another illegal whorehouse, in the beginning of the night. In a bit of a fishy neighborhood we go to a dirty bar filled with drunken regulars. It smells like old sweat, cigarette smoke and all kinds of nastiness. There are stray dogs barking in front, and broken glass lies spread out on the floor, that is sticky from all the spilled beer - it is generally not a nice place to be in, at all. In the back there is a dark smoke-filled hallway leading to an inner court with small sheds, transformed into workrooms big enough to hold one double bed. A bathroom compound where the filth is unmatched, has toilets that do not flush and most of the doors are missing. Cockroaches are everywhere. My heart breaks to see these poor conditions. Not to mention the earnings that to western standards are way below minimum wage. The pimp, leaning back on a wooden chair wearing a stained tank top with his chest hairs sticking out, gets his wringing twelve dollars for an hour. How much he actually gives to the girls nobody wants to share, likely out of shame.

What happens next are images I cannot forget. At least a dozen half naked girls suddenly run out to the poorly-lit streets, carrying their clothes between squeezed arms, and disappear into dark alleys of the early night. Reason for this is fear of being arrested and deported as two police cars pull over and a team of officers jump out! I stand in amazement as it all unfolds in front of my eyes. Flickering blue and red lights light up the whole scene. However, it is not for them - the police stormed into a house opposite the street for some drug related issue, trying to arrest some criminals. Perhaps they did not even know about the secret brothel. Understandably the girls cannot take the risk of waiting to find out. This night, creepy men are not the only ones being blown by the prostitutes; they also blow their own cover.

Just when you think you have seen it all, the night has more in store for me. Still bewildered by those slender half naked bodies that I have witnessed, I walk back to my hostel. This area feels far from safe as I notice thugs watching me, these cliché-looking figures of notorious Latino gangs. Angry eyes scout my every move. As always, I am on guard, it's one of the reasons why I never wear flip-flops at night. They do not make me feel secure. In fact, I don't go anywhere unless I am wearing shoes, may the time come to defend myself or in case I have to run.

Being literally two minutes away from my fenced-in hostel, assuming the situation is under control, things turn ugly. Out of nowhere, two guys are next to me on a bicycle. While one sits on front on the frame bar, they both jump off and pull a butcher knife on me! For a moment I'm staring death in the face. Actually, I'm staring at two faces, that both seem determined to shank me for a couple of nickels. Since they stand right in front of me, the situation does not allow for a kick or punch. In a nanosecond, I have to decide what to do. It amazes me to this day how clear my mind is. At least ten options pop up and I decide that avoiding contact is always the best option, now more than ever with my pockets filled with a cellphone and too much cash. I lean back like Neo in the Matrix, dodging bullets in slow motion, at least that is how I perceive it, and spurt away. For I know I can run like the wind. The knife pullers come to the same conclusion as they have a hard time keeping up while chasing me. When a taxi passes by I signal the driver to stop. Making eye contact, he must be thinking I am some kind of crackhead or something with that look upon my face, so he accelerates. Pumping with adrenaline I run so fast I actually manage to get beside him, pull the left back door open and make a risky move to jump into the moving vehicle! A woman sitting next to the driver looks at the backseat with a quenching face, startled about what this honky is up to. I just yell to keep on moving, explaining with a few words of Spanish that these guys are chasing me with a weapon. Luckily, the driver believes me and rushes to a nearby police post.

Here, two armed police officers are ready for action - they get on their dirt bike straight away to find the getaway perpetrators. Moved by compassion the driver makes the effort to drop me off in front of my hostel, not far from Plaza Alfonso López. Furthermore, he refuses to take money from me for the ride, making me not loose faith in the people. An old central Colombian saying says that what grows up crooked will never grow right. This counts for the guys that tried to mug me, or worse. What shall become of them?

Later that night I also gain trust in other people. Sitting in the courtyard beneath a starry sky to let it all sink in, I meet a French traveler who wears a classical hat with a feather. After telling my story my adrenaline level steadily starts to drop. All this time my limbs were still sort of tingling, only half realizing it could have had a different outcome, with me in the hospital or lying flat on a sidewalk with a tarp covering my dead body. Going around on a motorbike also, my fellow-European has squinting eyes and a charming voice when he speaks English with that accent. A character of epical proportions, you know, dressed with his shirt open with two buttons too many. We happen to share the same room and have the dormitory to ourselves. When it is bedtime, by now stoned out of his mind, he lights a thin white candle placing it on a wooden nightstand. Mind you that I, already in my underwear, have to get out of bed to blow it out. Even possibly preventing the room catching on fire, because Mister Frenchman fell asleep right away, demonstrated by a loud snore. What a peaceable moment.

Having come to my senses in the following days, it is time to survey the rest of the province. Bus rides are supposedly a pain in the ass to the village of La Mina, riding my own transportation is easy and pleasant. A couple of hours of hilly scenery is captivating as ever and the weather is outstandingly good. It is so remote that I have to fill up my tank with gasoline from plastic bottles. In the village, some men are selling them from under a tree, keeping the liquid in the shade - not a gas station in sight. The point of interest at the river *Rio Candela* are the eroded boulders, as far as I know the only ones in its kind. Indeed worth the visit.

By the time the day is over I know how it feels like to have a sixty-year-old German woman on the back of my motorcycle. With the highly unregulated public transport, the poor lady did not know how to return so she asked for a lift. I cannot help thinking it would have been more fun if she were forty years younger, but hey, I made someone's day, and that's what counts.

Back in the city of Valledupar an unforgettable memory begins at *Casa Indigena*. At this office where matters concerning the indigenous people are handled, I need to ask for permission to my next destination. An official reply from the tribe elders can sometimes take days. Visitors are denied more often than not. A talkative girl from Belgium joins me on this extraordinary adventure to where, according to oral traditions and legends, the sun was born. We are stunned, at least I am, to see a young lady in a tight orange dress and high heels between the traditional outfits of people from the *Arhuaco* tribe. Kinda hard to miss if you know what I mean. Turns out this beauty has some brains too as she is an attorney. Hired by an independent group she has taken up several complicated cases where she mediates between the government and the tribe. If that is not enough her heart is also in the right place. For the very next day she manages to fix us a ride to the secluded and forbidden lands.

We can actually join the supply truck that brings provisions every other week. Crammed in between smelly bags we leave at five in the morning. Straight roads gradually turn into bending ones going further uphill. At one point, we do not know if the mist is so high up or the clouds being so low. By the time we arrive in a two lane town called Pueblo Bello it's getting rather nippy, unknowingly having climbed in altitude. With first daylight we sit ourselves down to endure a tasteless breakfast, carrying on with a visit to the butcher for some fresh meat, to take it with us to the village with the little space left. This is no ordinary butcher. In one corner a man is bashing cow skulls with a huge axe, neatly saving the brains and eyes. In another corner thirteen-year-old boys are slicing the meat off carcasses with knives you wouldn't expect in thirteen-year-old hands! Dogs are walking around unhindered and sometimes an aluminum roller shutter in the middle section opens, where tuk tuks wait with running engines, right next to the fresh meat, filling the whole place with exhaust fumes.

When we continue our way we find out the rumors about the road to take were nothing less of exaggeration. It's so bad you literally wouldn't even consider this walkable. Let that sink in for a moment. Our four-wheel drive only broke down three times! It needed to get fixed on the spot. And an innumerable amount of times we got stuck or can't get uphill because the mud makes it too slippery. A regular car, or an inexperienced driver for that matter, wouldn't even last ten yards. Dense green hills, intense red dirt and view on the very distant Andes Mountains, hundreds of kilometers away, make up for the bumpy ride lasting all day. Shaken and stirred we penetrate the *Sierra Nevada* de Santa Marta. Extra permission from the elders of the tribe is necessary upon arrival at the first gates. For a moment we reckon our efforts and good intentions in vain after we undergo a visual examination by tribal guards. Then, by a miracle they grant us entry. Yet they watch every move with black distrustful eyes. And rightly so, too often outsiders have tried to oppose them.

Somehow, the settlers managed to keep their village exactly as it was as in the year 1915 (and probably decades if not centuries before that) as a framed black and white photo proves in the room pointed out for us to sleep in, having the date handwritten in the bottom-right corner. Truly their territory is a magical one. So untouched and pure, fully absent of any form of industrial revolution. Hiding between hills of green, stand grazing donkeys next to rocky creeks. Healthy pasture lands are bright in color. Here, wild boars are just boars, nothing wild about them. Animals have never been hunted by the *Arhuacos* so they don't feel threatened. Everyone is living in perfect harmony. Wandering around the area the realization sets in that this is a real-life fairytale. A mix of monumental forrest plants and tropical ones, all intertwined. White robes the residents are wearing contrasts their long black hair, that straightly rests along their broad red cheekbones like a shroud. Over-exposure to the sun has darkened their already dark skin. From generation to generation always one big cheek filled with coca leaves on which they chew all day long. This gets them into hallucinations of which one of them is their idea of superiority. They are the self-proclaimed *older brothers*, whilst the rest of the world, not yet enlightened as they are, are the *younger brothers*. Whatever works for them, right? At least we are brothers. Of course, I am talking about non other than the fascinating town of Nabusimake.

A final permission is needed to enter the walled village of their actual living space, where the houses are - constructed with uncut stone blocks from the riverbed and roofs of cane. Taking photographs is out of the question. First of all, the ground we stand on is holy to them, but understandingly they also seek to protect their ways. Thus, we try to stay in the background as much as possible. However, we do nod politely to the elders and say: "Hello, how are you?" in the *Arhuaco* language, that we learned five minutes prior to entering the camp, but is definitely appreciated. They have this respectful custom that whenever they meet one another it is mandatory to greet and put a handful of coca leaves into each other's *mochila*, which is a traditionally woven shoulder bag. I like that. Such a simple gesture, but with such major implications. As a unique moment in history we are allowed to witness a meeting with government officials, where further action is discussed concerning the matter of their holy mountain. Ever since it was confiscated without any negotiations the tribe is unable to perform their rituals. Today the green mountain even hosts an army base and cell towers. Trying to not offend anyone I can't help myself to make contact with the children. Offering to share food usually works, but making weird faces pulls them over the edge. Smiles are beautiful and their teeth still white, not yet spoiled by drugs the adults are all consuming, leaving an unappetizing layer. Men and women are mostly clutched in small groups sticking to their own sex.

The cute attorney from *Casa Indigena* that managed to get us here, is also present. As the women prepare the meat that we brought for a common meal, we get to know each other a bit. At the end of the meeting we both have the feeling we just might catch up sooner or later. As months go by, it turns out that feeling was right. But before racy details a whole lot of sightseeing.

Meanwhile I came back to civilization, or at least something that closely resembles one. Having hiked with the Belgium girl to the nearest village until the sun is about to set we coincidentally catch the last bus of the day. Although my final days in the green city are spent with good food, I have to make an extra hole in my waist belt. Going from here to there always makes me loose quite a bit of weight. An early leave takes me through desert plains with dead straight roads and hilled jungles with winding roads. When passing a traffic sign that warns for crossing monkeys I become aware of how far away from home I really am. On the motorcycle there is plenty of time to think about questions I ask myself, such as *What is home?* It is the place where I speak the language, have some friends, enjoy food that is nowhere else and where it is easy to make money. Other than this there is nothing that really binds me with the Netherlands.

Mere moments before sunset I reach picturesque Playa de Belén. Aside from a river there is no body of water to detect, so why they chose to incorporate the word 'beach' into the town's name is a grabber. All I see is a small Catholic village at the foot of a natural park. Cobblestone streets are mostly abandoned. Lichen is embracing electricity lines. Snugly houses in narrow alleyways are decorated with colorful lights owing to the approaching holidays. We are but a few weeks away from the pagan rituals of Christmas. Some residents, chitchatting in their doorways, don't return a 'Buenas noches' when I greet them. Well, suit yourself. *Enjoy that Mass at church with Christmas you sanctimonious hypocrites!* I think to myself as I walk by. Excuse me, I tend to take uncivilized behavior personally. I'm working on it.

During breakfast in the morning, sitting in the small restaurant section of some hotel (perhaps the only one?) the rest of the chairs remain empty. Business is awfully slow in the off-season. It is cloudy when I walk over to yet another area where one wonders what the heck must have happened at one time in the past. The marvelous wonders of this world proudly present the hills of *Los Estoraques*. Once washed away by an incredible force of water it has left remarkable stone pillars in red. It is powerful and a kind of mysterious too with a halo right above the towering rocks. As seems to be getting a habit of mine it is granted to walk completely by myself. Only a funny dog is tagging along. The black collie seems to like me and is occasionally asking for a tap. Dissimilar to the animal's happiness I keep finding shell casings of a large-caliber machine gun. I'm not sure what to make of it or what happened in bygone times. What I am sure about is the ceiling of clouds that breaks open in the afternoon. I wish I had brought sunscreen. Within the next days the intense sun caused the skin to peel right off my face. It was painful for a week and a half and I walked around with a red face for at least a month. It won't be the last time.

Landscapes constantly change from deserts to rainforests - what an exhilarating variety in sceneries! My body is cold from the rains that keeps on falling. Today is a day of tiering the asphalt before Bucaramanga is on the menu. Built on the highest hill in the region, the massive city rises out of the green as the modern capital of the Santander department. It is young, it is fast, and filled with students and fashionable stores, a bit oppressive after being so one with nature. I let my clothes hang to dry on the edge of my bunkbed in a hostel. Oh, how I yearn for a hot shower now. Not surprisingly, I have to do without - again.

Some well-deserved sleep on a good mattress gives enough strength to be on the move again. I don't feel like spending too much time in urbanized regions. After all, a city remains a city, while nature always finds a way to tantalize the senses. According to this App, called Mapsme, it is a five-and-a-half hour drive to my next destination. Spending a whole day on my AKT *Enduro* getting not even remotely close, a hotel in Malaga provides shelter. Good thing downloading that App is without any costs, for it couldn't be more inaccurate. Exhausted from the dangerous route I go to bed early. Driving off-road all day has drained me from all my energy. Dirt roads, bumps, potholes, and even parts of the road itself missing. At dawn I am facing the same craziness all over again alongside cliffs with the constant hazard of falling rocks, the chance of sliding on gravel roads, having to cross wild rivers and a staggering number of landslides. Clear views on valleys and mountains are immaculate, providing visual relief from the intensities I'm left facing every day anew.

Scents of trees and flowers are strong and unadulterated. I cannot stress enough how undisturbed it is. The pristineness is overwhelming to the core. Being so one with the earth brings suppressed emotions to the surface. It is as such less traveled that for the most part I have the road to myself. For hours and hours I come across no one. It is a form of art to learn that loneliness is not the same as the exquisite unsurpassed solitariness.

· · ·

Early in the afternoon on a Monday, the cozy village of Cocuy presents itself. I am at the foot of the Andes Mountains for the first time in my life. Men and women are both dressed with a woolen blanket over their daily outfit. Except for the youngsters everyone is wearing a hat, which is best described as a fusion between a bowler hat and a cowboy hat. For the most part I am ignored. In shops however, I receive a fair amount of smiles. In the center an army unit patrols a jolting square. As I walk by, they all stop and throw straight faces without saying a word, until I am out of sight. "That didn't feel threatening at all!" I sarcastically say to myself. Going about town a good ration is gathered for the big day of tomorrow.

To my disappointment, more or less twenty-four hours after I arrive, it turns out not to be that big of a day when I find the park closed off to the public. And with park I mean the humongous renowned Nature Preserves. To the southeast the snowy peaks of the *Devils Pulpit* and the *Diamond* are clearly visible by the time clouds resolve. I've hardly parked and locked my bike when I already spot a route where I can enter illegally. Then, three guards show up that surround me, fouling up any opportunity. They virtually don't leave my side until I depart after some hours on account of the rain. Of course, I know the parks are closed. Everyone has repeatedly warned me not to come here, especially with the ninety-nine percent chance of it being for nothing, plus all the trouble from dangerous roads. Yet I cannot allow myself to neglect this area and I cannot forgive myself if I have not at least given it a shot. There are rumors too, you know. There is this story, that if you're lucky to meet passing indigenous, you can try to make friends with them so they will allow you in, perhaps the only chance you have. I know myself too well - not trying would mean a nagging voice in the back of my head, haunting me and accusing me for months. I am not going to let that happen. Even not after this first failed attempt. Surely, I did not come all the way for nothing.

As soon as the next day I head towards the Andes Range via the village of Güicán. Despite horrible trails that are devastating for my motorcycle, because my tires are eaten alive and the whole thing pretty much rattles apart, the scenery of Kanwuara takes me back in time immediately. In fact, time must have been standing still for thousands of years. Another one of those unspoiled areas with wild horses, cattle that belongs to what seems desolate farms, tall evergreens, winding streams and birds of prey circling the stretched skies. Pen and paper cannot describe the innocence of the place with the purest of air flowing through my nostrils. Just when I begin to think I actually outsmarted the authorities by taking this route, the relish comes to an end at an unexpected check point, with a red and white barrier blocking the way. Bummer. However, this check point is very remote and as far as I can tell there is only one guard. In exchange of registration by name and passport number it is allowed to go to a nearby viewpoint uphill. This is what I was waiting for. This uniformed individual has to stay in his watchtower and can't be at two places at the same time, now can he? He receives a solemn promise I won't go beyond the rendezvous point, which is out of sight for him. Tackled the authorities after all. As soon as I am on top and turn around the corner, having bulges of land blocking his view, saving my ass if you will, I go full throttle and drive *way* beyond the location of our little agreement. Steering towards the eternal snow of Playitas I am treated to a full Andes skyline with over five-thousand-meter high summits! It is like having the whole world to yourself. Being above the tree-line there are no sounds, no animals, and nothing that disturbs the serenity. Passing the same guard on the way back, much later than anticipated, he knows from the smirk on my face he has been duped. But what can he do?

Returning to Cocuy an old man raises his hand, beckoning me to pull over. While I am wondering if he needs a ride he already climbs on the back on the side of the road. That is settled then. With my self-acquired three-week-old Spanish, we start a small conversation. He offers to pay me when he steps off in front of his house, bills of Pesos already in his hand. He is more dumbfounded than happy when I tell him to put it back into his pocket. Locking the door of my hotel room I slowly start preparing for the next trip. First, I warm up with a long longed-for hot shower in a cheap yet spacious private room. All this, when converted for only five euros. But the inconvenience is ironic. Finally steaming water while my painful sunburned skin still peels off. On top of that, because of the sudden change of weather I developed a cold sore on my upper lip. It is either the weather, or maybe, just maybe, I shouldn't have gone down on one of those girls from Venezuela.

And then there is the hilled city of San Gil, which costs me eleven hours of my life to get there. Including two near-death experiences, caused by reckless drivers. Entering the dirty city, known for its outdoor activities, the sun sets behind the green hills. In doing so creating an orange heaven over the districts divided by rich and poor. The last twenty miles on pavement are a treat; all day through the mountains has left me shudder, up to the point in a squeaky hostel bed at night. Not yet knowing I will end up in a hospital only a few days later, with much more shuddering on the way. Prior to one of the weirdest experiences I ever had, I try to rest for a few days and let my face get into its natural shape and form.

One of those outdoor activities is the actual reason for coming to the more centralized parts of the country. I don't care much about wild-water rafting or repelling, nor mountain biking or guided hikes. All fine, but of course this is the place to be for voluntarily running off a mountaintop and jumping into ravines! It may sound crazy but this is actually happening. Not without a parachute tied to your back though. I am speaking about the activity of paragliding! This one has been on the list for years. So why not do it where it is also very affordable? When the day has come to define the laws of nature, the white van of a safe and certified company takes groups of daredevils to a high top, all day through. With view over the *Chicamocha* Canyon I am about to take part in the miracle of human aviation. Blue skies have me excited as a kid in a candy shop. Nothing can ruin this day now. Or can it? When it's my turn I buckle up and fearlessly run off the mountain. Before I know it I soar like a bird in the open air. To convince myself I am not dreaming I repeatedly yell "I'm flying!" It is amazing how much control you have when directing your parachute. To not end up at the bottom of the Canyon, a mile lower, I have to circle about to gain altitude. In no-time I get giddy and nauseous. Within a minute I discover that my body is not made for this due to my congenital balance disorder. On top of this, my hyperventilation attack from yesterday (another thing that I suffer from since as long as I can remember) resumes and there goes my breakfast in mid air, from out of my abdomen. Out of safety it is a wise choice to return. After five minutes of heavy breathing I make a perfect landing whilst remaining fully conscious, but not for long.

Finding myself a spot to relax I intent to wait for thirty minutes. That is usually how long it takes to recover from this condition, that somehow continued after childhood. By the time a French traveler asks me how long I think I am already on the ground, things get weird. With his phone he confirms my presumed ten minutes are now two hours! I don't remember anything. As the very helpful French guy is pondering what to do next, I loose my speech. In my head I make correct sentences but when I try to put it into actual words nothing but gibberish comes out. I am thinking *Okay, this is starting to get somewhat worrisome.* Suddenly my hands begin to cramp up, my fingers turn crooked as if I am having an attack, best described as spasms. I have no idea what is happening to me. My mind is clear and because of my curiosity I am actually consciously interested of how this one will turn out. Several attempts to walk have failed dramatically. As soon as I open my eyes I get so extremely dizzy that my diaphragm tenses up and violently tries to pull everything out of an already empty stomach. By now the van with which we came has long left, together with the other participants. One company member and the French guy stick around and arrange a taxi for me and them, or so I hear later. Have you ever seen that scene from the movie *The Wolf of Wall Street,* where an overdosed Leonardo tries to crawl into his Ferrari from off the ground? Well, that is how I get into the car, somehow able to climb in the backseat. It takes ages, and once going I vomit uncontrollably due to the traffic, that constantly makes the car stop and pull up again.

With my face in a bag we arrive at the hospital where they examine me, after waiting ridiculously long in a wheelchair in the hallway. Still heavily breathing, not being able to open my eyes nor speak. According to the test results my blood and blood pressure is all fine. After some more testing, the doctors come up with the only thing they can possibly think of. Apparently, I suffer from a mosquito virus! They prescribe a bunch of medicine of which they strongly recommend to take them on the appropriate times. Later that night I pick them up at the pharmacy. When I check up on those three days later, I am flabbergasted to find out I had been taking ordinary vitamin pills and paracetamol! Like that does anything and like I didn't already have those with me in the first place. They basically didn't do shit about the recovery process or to find out what the actual cause is. But I am still alive, and up to this day it never happened again.

Days go by as the dizziness is hardly receding. In the course of time, pig-headed as I am, I install my gear on the motorcycle in the early morning hours and take off. My spirit is in dire need of refilling my recommended daily allowance of adventurous activities. Marvelous lands make me forget about my unhealthy situation. As well as the pain in my bottom for sitting all day long on a dirt bike. This machine is not built for driving the entire continent. Which actually starts to look like I am busy doing. It is long dark before I check-in into a hotel in Puerto Boyaca, a mediocre city situated next to the wide Magdalena River, admired because of her length of almost a thousand miles! Call it coincidence, call it fate, call it whatever you want, but the cute attorney from *Casa Indigena,* who is living in Bogotá herself, has a mother in this town that she so happens to be visiting. I know, right? What are the chances? You guessed it, the next day I check out of the hotel and experience some good old Colombian hospitality.

Her mother is a very friendly lady. Since she has a boyfriend that lives only one block away, it makes her practically live there. Long story short, the attorney and I have the house to ourselves. Therefore it does not take long for us to get to know each other a little better and at least two times a day a lot better. It does seem the girl and I are fond of each other. With her taking some time off from work we have an opportunity to explore the area, and what better way to combine that with exploring one another also? On one of these occasions we end up at a deserted waterfall, where the water at the bottom gently crushes into a breathtaking blue lagoon in the midst of the overgrown jungle with fitting temperatures, essentially putting its seal on the already unreal setting. *How is this place not completely bombarded with tourists?* I wonder. Hazy rays of sunshine making it through the dense verdure, extra visible due to moist in the air, reveal a big rock with flat surface right next to the lagoon. It takes little imagination what you could do if ending up in a situation as perfect as that.

Satisfied with new experiences, we drive back and pass *Hacienda Nápolis,* a big track of real estate, formerly owned by the notorious drug lord Pablo Escobar. At the entrance of the theme park I am amused to find a one-engine airplane that is placed on an arch above the road, and not just any airplane, it was the first one used in a long record of flights, smuggling drugs into the United States. And we all know how it went from there. Fun fact: when you drive passed the parking lot you end up at a diversion. Turning right, the way leads towards the actual zoo that is a part of the park, going left, you go to another kind of zoo, the Penitentiary Institution. I can only imagine the burden of new inmates driving up and seeing all those happy families and day-tourists enjoying their free time. Something they won't have until they get out. Speaking about Escobar's animals - what to do if you like hippopotamuses and you have an endless supply of wealth? That is right, you import a few of those into South America and have them roam your property. When the regime fell, the last men leaving that property thought to themselves the big creatures would probably go extinct in no-time, without taking care of them. Little did they know, the animals would mate like crazy! Decades later resulting in the large population of hippopotamuses as it is today. And that is as funny as it is remarkable, the animals in no way being native to these green expanses of hispanic ground.

When I relaunch my expedition I get to meet more locals with big hearts, hence, my days are filled with wonderful times. I get invited to a *finca*, which is basically a huge track of land with stables, horses, and cows with that typical bump on their backs. I learn that my host, that I can call uncle, rents a small empire of four square kilometers in total. This is more like it; fresh milk from the cows, howler monkeys as well as sloths in subtropical trees, and macaws doing fly-bys. Sometimes I really meet the right people at the right time. Herding livestock on horseback for days, all the while wearing a cowboy hat, certainly is a lifestyle I can get used to. Perhaps the only tough job is when we have to push one group of cows into a certain outside run, and a second group of cows into another, using bare hands. But that is still more of a hobby than work to me. The farmyard has a separate house which I have to myself. All day long I am being fed by the lovely wife of uncle, who prepares the best dishes in her kitchen, such as the traditional *tamales*. To say that I am moved by their openness would not do it justice. Their unconditional hospitality, combined with all the animals and riveting terrain, makes me feel at home more than I initially realize.

Going from one village to another, more invitations are spontaneously thrown into my lap. In one of those cases, I receive the ultimate inauguration by meeting the whole family, around Christmas time. A little too soon for my taste, but welcome to Latin traditions I suppose. Each house I visit has presents in shiny gift-wrapping for everyone. *Un poco* uncomfortable as I have not celebrated this manmade holiday for about fifteen years. In the following days, my newly aquatinted friends and I, delight in all kinds of activities and occasionally together with the extended family. Apart from taking a boat-ride on a motorized canoe across the river, being out of my comfort-zone, we go out for a feisty lunch next to a swimming pool in a small nearby village. Usually, these types of gatherings involving food are funded by the same individual, who does not allow for anyone else to pay the bill. Beyond kindness, it seems more like an issue of pride, as some men find it hard to step over that obsolete *macho* behavior. To show gratefulness for all they have done I like to do something in return. Having our tummies filled, they object against me paying but I beat them to the punch, even stirring some commotion because of it.

On New Year's Eve, some of us, including me, are kitchen bound - we prepare food all evening in the form of fruit salads and several local dishes. After the mundane countdown, when the clock hits twelve, I am actually too tired to eat but I do not object to participate in the traditional practice of eating twelve grapes, while doing twelve wishes. Mind you, this has to be completed within one minute. Now *that* is a race against time. Given they are all too animated with stuffing their cheeks, no one notices that I call it a night, after eating only five or six pieces. Who believes in these superstitious things anyway?

All together I am dressed in a cloak of new experiences. You can say what you want about these crazy Latinos, they sure know how to make one feel welcome. With temperatures below zero in my own country, I simultaneously revel in the healing strata of thirty degrees Celsius. What an eventful way to end the year and start a new one!

4

COLOMBIA - SAGA DOS

A climate that gives you a bronze-golden tan for free, swinging music bounces around people-filled streets, freshly squeezed mango juice for a nickel 'n dime, and every day is a field day with so many pretty *chica's* around. In spite all these beckoning attributes, I would have never guessed it, but in a turn of events I return to Colombia seven months later at the very end of the trip, mainly to take care of some unfinished business for another month. Before we continue with the main story line, allow me to describe, in a nutshell, some of the ways I spent my time in the northern parts of this diverse society with addictive features.

After an aircraft drops me off once more in the city of millions, with an incomprehensible magnitude almost solely fostering distress, called Bogotá, I can't seem to escape quick enough. This capital won't be missed. Two cheap domestic flights that are taking me to the sun-drenched Caribbean is a huge relief, this is more or less the uplifting location from where I set off on my AKT motorbike. The plaguing annual typhoons cause one flight to delay for half the day but I couldn't care less. I do care however, that my air pilots of later that day are just as lousy as the cab drivers down below. Apart from the sheer phobia this shaky flight induces, taking very deep breaths is the only remedy against the nauseousness. Once safely there, the humid smells feel pleasantly familiar and all is forgotten.

How to better spend your time than legitimate island hopping on tropical islands? Isla Fuerte, to start with, is known for its white sand beaches and easeful bays. The string attached is that the only way of getting there is by boat. Once I induced myself to climb aboard are the waves too high to get seasick, lucky for me, and due to our high rate of speed way too hard as well, making the bones of my bottom rattle on the polyester seats. Throughout the island you can rent romantic cabañas in dense jungles, and right on the dream-like coast. Though nowadays you can find a place to sleep almost anywhere. Upon realizing that there was money to be made, ambitious locals are offering their own houses as accommodation, giving the resorts some competition.

On an exploring walk I run into a man who volunteers to take me to Morgan's Cave, an actual hidden cave in a banana plantain, hewn out from the soft bedrock. If that doesn't make you feel like the old pirates going treasure hunting I don't know what will. My impromptu guide is going about barefoot, and he is wearing a frayed rope around his worn-out pants, functioning as a belt. His dark brown skin is marked with deep furrows, far removed from vanity, grey facial hairs stick out here and there, making him such a beautiful character. Ensuring his donkey doesn't run off, using a thick leather cord to tie the stubborn animal to a picket fence, he goes on to show me around.

An invitation to his house follows, which is literally built from scratch and almost falling apart. It seriously looks like it was thrown up from washed up materials. Even an old plastic lawn chair gets to keep its value, needle and thread inventively sewed the tearing of the broken parts back together. I mean, stitching up a plastic chair, seriously? When a huge boar comes waggling by, not sure if he owns the gluttonous thing, it carelessly spades through the smelly dirt. In all his poverty, the man does own two guanabana trees, and he is happy to share the delicious fruits with me. It is always nice to meet people with a heart way bigger than their wallet.

One of the other Caribbean islands is called Múcura. Now there's a place to remember for when you are retired, for what an astounding piece of paradise this is. The sound of the wind caressing the big leaves of many palm trees lift's anyone's spirit, together with other exotic plants they are scattered across light green fields, so bright it almost looks tasty. For the aquatic lovers there are turquoise bays with shallow waters that are ideal for snorkeling. With a set of goggles with air tube the treasures of the veiled deep are revealed. Between the coral there are starfish, stingrays, and little bright colored fishes, the last ones are being hunted by pelicans that are scouting every suspicious move. I enjoy the wooden pole cabañas with waterproof palm leaf roofs, in fact, I rented one of those, and further enjoy the spun up hammocks, and the intense sun all day long.

Life is good here, and if you're opting for optimal enjoyment, it is better to wear sunblock to cover your face and shoulders, otherwise you might end up as red as one of the many jolly crabs residing on the island. They are literally everywhere, one time I even had to chase them out of my outdoor shower compartment! Top notch tranquility with daily fresh grilled fish from the sea, straight onto your plate. Inhabitants are friendly yet in general they like to be left alone. Nosey children on their turn couldn't be dragged away, and love to engage in conversation with foreigners. For maximum serenity you might want to avoid the months of December and January, when it is most visited. Altogether, hardly anyone passes these waters without checking out the trendy nearby attraction of *Casa de agua,* which is more or less a floating party mansion, where the alcohol affluently flows, and the first day in history still has to appear where they don't possess marihuana.

Not afraid of some action? At a nearby lesser-known Caribbean island there is more entertainment. It is possible to hire a guy that will single-handedly peddle you there with a rowboat. May you endure the open waters and reach it after an hour or so you can pet tamed sharks, witness bioluminescent plankton at night, making you feel as if you are trapped in the movie *Avatar* itself, or visit the animating mangrove with intertwined roots well above the water surface. Seek no further for a place with maximum leisure.

I cannot think of a better way to end my three hundred sixty-five day trip. Having seen a whole lot of stuff I can say with hand on my heart it is effortless to fall in love with Colombia, a country that is inspirational in so many ways. But first, returning to our lead story, there is a whole lot of uncharted land to cover on my brand new motorcycle.

Extended greenish croplands, characterized by their serenity and simplicity, are replaced by large meandering hills that are getting more elevated by each passing kilometer marker. Movement on the roads is increasing by the minute, as well as the pollution that they are collectively responsible for. In the first days of the new year an endless string of vehicles is impatiently waiting in line, they are proof that the next cultural hot spot is advancing.

Starting with a distinct one, that needs no introduction to most people: Medellín, home of the infamous Pablo Escobar. More and more perceptible, especially since the launch of the Netflix series *Narcos*. Whereas Colombia has South America's finest women, rumor has it that this second largest city is the place to be for the *country's* finest women. Only a few decades ago you did not want to be here as at least ten murders a day were committed. Brutal street shootings, knife attacks, and gruesome killings became mundane things. It was no surprise when buildings in crowded shopping centers were blown up, totally disregarding human life – people can remember it all too well. In fact, it has left such a mark that even today it is not allowed for two guys to ride on the same dirt bike together. Namely, this particular vehicle was almost always used during these violent quick attacks and served as quick getaways, severely feared by the general public. Nowadays the atmosphere is totally different with none of that type of action. Well, a little perhaps, with the exception of the abundance of cocaine and cheap prostitutes. In that sense, little has changed since the former days of glory.

Many backpacker hostels offer free walking tours, though they are never really free in the end. Shame was written on the faces of the tour guides when they begged for money, stating that showing us around was deserving of a little contribution. Speaking of which, if you have made it this far you cannot deny yourself to go on an Escobar tour, as the next little excursion is called. Meaning driving along buildings he owned, viewing the house where he was shot, and visiting his grave on a large cemetery with a splendid *vista* across the hazy city. Mixed feelings arise when I see people still showing adoration to this mass murderer by laying flowers to glorify his legacy. That is the power of propaganda right there. Still, it was very informative to see the apartments he blew up. Furthermore, it is quite impressive for his time period that he was able to utilize highly progressive communication systems with massive satellite dishes and huge palm trees that he had imported from Miami. Believe it or not, but you can actually visit his brother and take a picture with this guy, of course indirectly sponsoring the old regime. I will skip it for now.

Semi trucks look like modern day gypsy caravans with an arched tarp, stretched over convex tubulars. A bit like what you see in the old western cartoons. White and yellow taxicabs are equipped with big stickers on the side doors showing their license plate. Locals warn me to better take an official one instead of one of the many Ubers around, if you don't want to risk ending up being woozy by a rag of chloroform with your belongings misappropriated. I even meet people who actually had that happening to them.

The climate is mild and as the rumors indeed promised there are gorgeous women. Both being very enjoyable they are not the main reason of sojourning to this urban jungle as I need to have my visa extended with urgency. In spite of my appointment at noon sharp, that previously took many hours of illogical online mandatory preparation, my turn comes at five o'clock in the afternoon. My behind has turned into mahogany from the uncomfortable chairs and now I have to repeat everything I already did online. After filling out a bunch of papers my fingerprints are taken also. Therefore, on the last legal day in the country, as a matter of fact in the last legal hours, a three-month extension is granted, and with that I am spared from a whole lot of complications.

Cruising over reasonable pavement my tail-heavy motorbike is still performing well, yet there are always reasons that prevent me to go on; up ahead a landslide has buried the road. Truly, the amount of collapsing hills are as numerous as the stars in the night sky. Twenty minutes before arriving in Medellín I had the same thing happening to me and now it is happening again. Just like then, this particular one forces me to take a big detour also, except now I'm heading toward a paradise in the swamplands called Guatapé.

Compared to the other way, the one I had laid out on my roadmap, this alternative route is genius. Wood stove smells enrich the air, green hills are filled with dense pine trees and little wooden houses, artisanal built. Everywhere dark wooden shops are selling statues and wood cutting arts. Quirking roads eventually lead to the middle- and upper-class areas of Guatapé, well known for its outstanding monolith. In the middle of flowing marshlands there stands this huge piece of granite rock named *El Piñol*. I blend into the flock of tourists from all over the world. Ascending the mortared brick stairs, with over seven hundred steps, you will be delighted with the view. From this point, one can see so many bodies of water, otherwise impossible to spot from the ground. Sunlight produces tantalizing colors, this is yet another place stirring the senses.

In the bathroom of a randomly chosen hostel, I find the same peculiar thing as in the rest of the country, the so-called suicide shower. It's a God granted miracle that no one is electrified to death with those copper wires sticking out! Where have I seen *that* before?

After being revived by lively nature and good cheap meals there's a two-day drive on my improvised schedule. Unfortunately, I must by now indefinitely leave the preferred climate behind. It is necessary to wear rain gear all day as rain can come out of nowhere in the mountains. Arriving in the suburbs of the big city, I spend one night in a small Catholic town called La Vega. Ending up in a home with a nice family with kids they feel obligated to show me around, and so it happens. The streets and the square in front of a typical Latin church are still lit up by thousands of little lights with the holiday just weeks behind us.

When time has come to enter old friend Bogotá, a place I'd reckoned to never see again, the massiveness of it all chokes me right away. It is something like having the opposite of claustrophobia in such big cities. The high buildings are extremely dense and there is an insane amount of traffic with unimaginable pollution. Cars sway dangerously from left to right and vice versa. I actually say out loud to myself "What a fucking hellhole!"

Having been in the purity of nature so recently, this new reality is a shock to the system. Who would have thought, I put myself through all of this, only for a reunion with the cute attorney who lives in the center. Understandingly our time is satisfying.

With her efforts pursuing her career, at one point she takes a plane to the other side of the country leaving me to spend the last days in the Metropole by myself. Making the most out of it, I meet up with another traveler I had met up north, who now happens to be volunteering here. Being alone and far away from home, meetings like this can really feel as if I am seeing a good friend again. Catching up we enjoy some conventional dishes such as *Patacones,* made from those big green bananas in a restaurant on Carrera 7, one of the main roads going straight through the city.

On my final day a sparse number of drops make their way down from the grey clouds in the sky. Trying to stay alive in the insane traffic jams, slaloming on my unpacked versatile bike for about a good hour out of the center, I am on my way to pay my respect to the majestic *Catedral de Sal*.

This religious accommodation is worth driving through the rain for, as the weather is significantly worsening. It is basically an old salt mine which has been transformed into a church with colorful lights and statues of angels. Evidence of some skilled industrious labor is all around. Gigantic crosses are cut out from the underground rock, among them the biggest in the world; the things humankind is capable of creating. Having spent some good hours in the tunnels I treat myself to a nice juicy steak. Restocking the energy levels is a frequent necessity.

Roads that are best described as ones that can strike constant fear of getting a flat tire, take me to the next destination. Questionable bridges, deep ravines with wild rivers, gravel roads and constantly scouting for the right route, make it into a full day drive. Steadily the dry soil turns reddish, held together by unending fields of wild cactuses. Powerful outlooks upon infinity are broken off in the far distance by contours of the mountains, just a slight complexion darker than the sky itself. Rays of the orange sun send a mystical glare on the red pillars of the *Tatacoa* Desert. It is a fascinating place where you can easily spend some days. It's like a smaller version of the Grand Canyon. You can go about hiking or horseback riding, and when you are not captivated by this natural pearl, or afraid of snakes and lizards, it is a perfect place to get inspired anew.

It also has an observatory that is open to the general public at night. Well, actually the observatory itself is closed to private individuals, but in the courtyard of the facility they organize star gazing events. Through two big telescopes they claim to have zoomed in on Venus. It looks nothing like what I have seen before through other telescopes, in fact, this looks more like a pre-recorded video of the moon, but what do I know, right?

On an outdated screen they show us computer generated images of planets, artist renditions of far away galaxies and all other things not observable to the human eye. Being fascinated by this for years in an almost obsessive way, I ask some challenging scientific questions to the employees who, as it turns out, are ill prepared to answer. They have a hard time evading them as I keep pressing to provoke a reaction. I can be a dick sometimes, although now it is just a harmless little game. As other visitors become increasingly stimulated for real answers, the employees on government payroll actually become too uncomfortable at one point and declare that the presentation has come to an end. You can't make this stuff up. I always liked the phrase *truth doesn't fear investigation*, but with their attitude it is indisputable they are trying to hide something.

On the way south I am struck by a gust of impulsiveness, causing me to change course and divert sideways for a few hours, leading up to days. It would be a shame to omit ancient archeological sites of pre-Colombian culture of the San Augustin area, that I just discovered by accident while checking for directions on my navigation device. Fully intact statues of humanoids and weird looking creatures are always fascinating. Let alone their highly advanced stone cutting techniques with laser precision cuts that leave our modern-day specialists speechless.

At the spontaneously chosen hostel in the hilly village, the owner, wearing goat hair sandals, supplies me with free marihuana right upon entry. Aha, that explains the group of unkempt hippies on the terrace, getting stoned for free! I decline however, for I have never smoked in my life and I tend to keep it that way. That goes for any type of cigarettes for that matter. I already inhaled enough smoke as a kid at family birthday parties in choking living rooms, or in the backseat of my parent's car with zero ventilation and the windows shut, where I was told to stop whining after having pulled the collar of my sweater half over my face from nearly suffocating. Thanks again there for the asthma! You gotta love the eighties when no one gave a tinker's damn, not even about something as harmful as smoking during pregnancy.

Anyway, the good man on goat hair sandals also knows a guy that organizes *special tours*, he says while holding up both index and middle fingers in nodding manner, where one can visit one of Escobar's former cocaine producing chemists. Surely, it is not a daily experience to partake in the entire process from plant to powder. As expected, you can also participate in testing the end result at the end of the day. By their own admission, two funny Germans staying at the same hostel had a good time during the tour. This Latin nation is not only saturated with cocaine, amazingly it also still thrives on it.

Listening at night to the congregated hippies, who are consistently high as a kite, cracks me up. They all talk slower than a drooling mentally challenged person. One of them gets my attention when he mentions how he was kicked out of his girlfriend's mother's house. Sloppy hair hanging down his face he goes on to explain how he had to survive in the woods by eating tree bark, which according to him, is pretty nutritious. I can't hold it any longer and burst into loud laughter when one of the other hippies replies to his story with the most passive voice ever "Yeah dude … trees are awesome."

Fun and games have definitely ended when going to Mocoa. The road is outright bad and the pavement is crumbling apart just by looking at it; in fact I have to manage my speed given the amount of cracks and potholes on the surface. Mocoa is another one of those areas that is plagued by landslides during these wet seasons. Not knowing that barely a month later Mother Nature will strike so hard it causes over three hundred deaths. That gives you an idea of how crappy everything looks and how poorly their houses are maintained. Once I passed the last traffic sign the road not only gets worse, it also stops existing! What's left is more or less a gravel trail. Locals have nicknamed it the *Trampoline of death* and this is because cars bounce off of one of the many cliffs on a regular basis. Coincidentally and sadly I get to witness one of these moments. At one of the very, very few curves that actually has a guardrail, a driver manages to go straight through it! Tumbling down the steep hill until it ends upside down in a rocky riverbed with a loud *bang*. It appears surviving family members have yet another crucifix to plant, as many other crucifixes are decorating this trail already, if you allow me to use that word, for lack of a better alternative.

Deep holes, filled up with murky rainwater are camouflaged by the same colored dirt road. Curves are unprotected, it is bumpy and my bladder is shaken so much that I have to pee every ten minutes. A few times my motorcycle slides away but my guardian angels allow me to stay in vertical position. My failing rain gear in these pouring showers isn't helping either. On top of that, my body is cooling down fast at these altitudes. With clouds all around, icy water is attacking from all sides. On a lot of places, the road is too narrow for two cars to pass. When they do meet one of them has to back up to a safe spot. Trucks and four-wheel drive jeeps almost push me over the edge at times. Not OK! Local drivers have zero patience and own this tendency to never yield. And it doesn't end there. Four or five times I have to cross through waterfalls of about a foot deep, if not more. A pretty strong current makes it exciting but not in a good way. Due to the white water there's no telling of what lies beneath, as in, obstructing pebbles and the like. Everywhere there are traces of preceding landslides with humongous dimensions, where bulldozers had to clear the road. The hazard for new ones is constantly there, as well as falling rocks and debris, especially in this weather. Every biker knows that not being focused on the road or losing concentration even for one second can be fatal. Without a doubt the worst five hours of my four months in Colombia. Well, not taken into account my admission to the hospital earlier on.

That night I am the only guest in a freezing hotel in the dead-end town of San Francisco. After a tasteless yet inexpensive hamburger, I make some small talk with shop owners, located around the square, where I buy some new socks. I amaze myself how I can communicate for a full hour with the few words of Spanish I know. As in other places where I linger for more than five seconds here also they try to hook me up to a woman, a single mother in this case, who cannot take her eyes off this cracker, apparently desirable wherever I place my foot. I am too tired to be interested. When it is long dark I walk the empty streets back to my hotel in the brightness of celestial beings in the sky. Simultaneously it becomes visible those beings, being the crescent moon, mars and venus, are having a hen party. Their rare closeness must be some sort of sign.

Trying to dry my wardrobe proves to be quite the task. I couldn't prevent my backpack leaking through, so now everything I have hangs out across the room. Clothes, towels and underwear are spread out on the broken radiator, on doors of an old cherry wooden closet, and on the edge of the bed. Being below ten degrees Celsius, my plan only half succeeds, a guarantee for a smelly backpack. It will take days to dry but I convince myself I have no time to waste, the road calls for more attention. This same road gets interestingly dangerous with ravines through mountains engulfed with thick clouds, and cliffs with serious overhang above me from where I'm driving. My motorcycle knows we are climbing as it cannot go beyond the annoying and frustrating second gear due to the thin air.

As the white sleek-lined layers of moist ascend out of the valley in the distance, they unfold the entire ramparts of the creative city of Pasto, that translates as *Pasture*. Endless fields of green about does the name justice and beautiful hills satisfy the retina with neat rectangular patches. As I am thinking of other places I have skipped, just as I am going to do with this one now, you might want to stop in the city of Cali, being an artistic bulwark, if you don't want to risk missing out on anything. Contrary to this one I *do* regret not visiting beautiful Salento, better known as the coffee area, to snap a photo of the tallest palm trees in the world, at *Valle de Cocora*.

For my last days in this wonderful country I arrive in possibly one of its ugliest cities. It knows nothing to be applauded for. The border-town of Ipiales truly is a gloomy aim. Somehow the dusty streets have a bad vibe to them but I can't quite put my finger on what it is. At an outdoor garage with chest high concrete walls the workmen clean and fix my bike for peanuts. Two guys with their hands covered in black grease convey a big smile when they ask me how long it took to drive from the Netherlands to here. Those guys probably played hooky during geography class, if they have ever seen a classroom from the inside to begin with.

On a visit to the consulate of Ecuador, to be prepared, the women inside let me know to arrange legal papers at the border itself. I am ready to get out of here as fast as I can, thus trying to neatly arrange everything on account of preventing any possible delay. Although I can't afford to miss one last thing.

Only six kilometers away lies the century old pilgrimage site of *Las Lajas*. Unique in its kind, this Cathedral could've undoubtedly been taken out from a scene of *The Lord of the Rings*, for it looks like *Minas Tirith*. Built as if it were sticking out of a rock with tall arches, white towers and a platform that forms a high bridge over a semi wild river that runs at the bottom of the valley. Hundreds of years of visitors has left a wall of plaques on the rocks with inscribed names and dates. Angelic statues on small pillars in the corners are keeping an eye on them. A roofed shrine with steps inside, displaying a surplus of candles, is so diligent that it starts to blaze. Two buckets of water carried by a robe wearing monk extinguishes the hell fire, causing liquid candle wax to fill tile joints while thick clouds of black smoke rise towards the swallows flying above. Even though it's evident to the trained eye that the nearby waterfall is fabricated, it fits in with the spiritually encumbered green hills. This is one to put on your bucket list.

Deified saints painted largely on the walls seem to pour their blessings onto me. Whispering I may continue in peace and all is forgiven. A perfect reconciling ending to all the craziness.

5

ECUADOR

Where did I end up this time? *De facto*, a place where women haven't yet received the illumination that wearing cheap leggings whilst being overweight produces an obvious camel toe. Or, being on the subject anyway, that wearing anything white, pants and tops alike, reveals white thongs and bras beneath them. Either they don't know or don't care, but there sure are plenty of them. When people want your attention in the market place, or even in restaurants, instead of saying *hello* or *hi* in their own language they make hissing sounds. Unimaginable in western society and totally unacceptable, there is a whole lot of hissing going on until they finally start calling out. Usually I adapt to cultural standards and assimilate out of respect; however, I refuse to partake in this uncivilized melodious habit. Even when you are born into this you must realize at some point, at least in my stubborn mind, how rude this can be to people from another culture. Not that I am offended in any way, don't get me wrong, I just don't bother to turn when they hiss at me.

Upon entry I am somewhat tense because I am not sure I possess the right documents. For example, not having a driver license for a motorcycle might not work for them. Soon enough it turns out all my worries were for nothing. My well-arranged insurance papers and identification gets me flawlessly across the border, albeit three and a half hours later, due to tourists that do have issues to cross. With the exception of Ipiales where I just came from I miss Colombia instantaneously. Yet at the same time my head is in the clouds of excitement, followed by an unfortunate overspread of actual clouds, getting darker by the minute. The fact that it has started raining cannot take away my enjoyment of the smoothly paved roads. My black dirt bike's suspension seems even happier than myself about this relief. Chaotic sub-cities and winding mountain roads take me to the northern parts of the capital, named Quito, five straight hours from the border on. During check-in at a hotel, that I happen to pass along the way, I wonder why the owner has this strange look on his face. About two days later I figure it out. There are only couples, or pairs at least, that check out after being inside for a mere hour. It is more or less a whorehouse. Usually I am quite sharp on these things but this one totally escaped me. How could I have guessed? Pretty much every woman that walks in, is as average as can be without stiletto heels or excessive make up.

Another long-held dream is fulfilled on my first full day in the country. Destiny has led me to visit *La mitad del Mundo,* which translates to "The middle of the Earth". Sure, the five-kilometer-wide equator runs through more countries in the world, but no other takes as much pride in it as Ecuador does. They even named their country after it, and, innumerable companies have the globe as their logo. The large obelisk-shaped monument towers the square and surrounding green fields. Along the walkway stands thirteen stone busts of the Masonic French surveyors who located this spot. Greatly neglected is the fact that they made a mistake, because the actual center of the equator lies two hundred and fifty meters away! However, the government has spent a lot of money putting this attraction on the map, no pun intended, and built a small town around it for the sole purpose of tourism. Relocating is not an option for semi-obvious reasons.

Within the dark tower there is an informative museum as well as an interactive museum where the public can perform all kinds of scientific tests that propagate the heliocentric model. Legend has it that this is the spot where the alleged northern hemisphere crosses over in the southern hemisphere. In spite of earth's supposed spin going at an astounding four hundred kilometers per hour faster than the speed of sound, adding up to a total of a staggering one thousand miles per hour at this exact location, it seems pretty motionless to me. But why would you trust your own senses if we can worship the masterminds of modern science with blind obedience?

The world's self-proclaimed highest capital is definitely an okay city. Although the newer more modern districts are worth visiting, what really makes the place striking are the hilly streets of the old part, overlooked by a shiny forty-five-meter-high aluminum statue of the Madonna. Masquerading the pagan traditions, this so-called Virgin of Quito is erected over an old sun worshipping temple. Furthermore, you can find a good lunch for two dollars everywhere and things are relatively cheap in general. Besides the disturbing outfits that certain chubby females are wearing, exposing too much of their skin, some women wear bright traditional tunics, man and women alike wear classical brown and black hats. Wandering around town reveals beautiful churches ordained with gold, marble, woodcuttings and statues of all the saints. Other religious structures shine because of their detailed paintings and massive stained-glass windows. You will be in awe in the Church of Saint Francis from all the diligent artwork. And for those taking an interest in gothic architecture the gutter outlets of the *Basilica del Voto* come in all sorts of animals.

Of the close to seven billion souls in the world I run into a Dutch acquaintance of mine in the big square. Besides going to a music concert in Germany together once, we don't know each other that well. With freshly squeezed mango juice we talk about our travel experiences in the sunshine. It is nice to speak in my own language again, which I hadn't done for a while. It is extraordinary how many people eat ice cream, I can't recall seeing that anywhere else. Also, it is advisable for non-vegetarians and meat eaters like myself to skip the KFC, it is absolutely horrible. I cannot believe it takes me two meals to realize that, taken into account that local dishes are so much better. Speaking of skipping meat, the provocatively dressed prostitutes congregating on street corners are downright ugly. Some of them are transvestites, but their cheap make-up does a poor job in hiding that. They wink, they whistle and don't hesitate to call after you. At least with me, for a gringo is good business. Some are bold enough to whisper nasty things into my ear as I pass. I smile at them and throw an occasional flirt in to mess with their minds.

With domestic elections approaching there is never a dull moment. Rallies and demonstrations fill up shopping streets with placards and huge banners, backed by loud music, which is closer to obnoxious noise instead of music. While sharing a bench with a long-haired hippie from the same hostel, we watch it all unfold before our eyes. There is so much to see. We crack up when roaming vendors approach with stolen shopping carts and start selling the craziest products. Laundry pins, phone chargers, combs, nail clippers - and who needs super glue all the time? Some individuals haggle for something that looks like ice cream cones but really isn't. The only usable item I detect is a bag of coca leaves. Once back at the cozy hostel, it is almost impossible to push my bike in due to a narrow doorway and a high threshold. After adjusting my exterior mirrors, a small pile of timber does the trick, put there by the friendly owner who assists me every time. In the kitchen, where an occasional cockroach rushes across the counter to hide in a stack of plates, we boil the natural leaves in a pan to enjoy the invasive taste of coca tea. To say that this beverage provides a delicious flavor would be an overstatement but it sure keeps me awake for the rest of the day. By the way, if you boil anything, be sure to use bottled water instead of tap water if you value your health, in spite of what locals tell you.

Since the beginning of time I have been a lover of tea. With appropriate shame, I confess I even catch a Starbucks sometimes to treat myself to a big Chai tea Latte - my goodness that stuff is addictive. Additionally, it always brings me back in memory to my endeavors in certain parts of Asia, where it was on the menu daily due to it being a common drink over there. On one of these occasions at the worldwide franchise, I meet a dazzling national beauty, a few years younger than I am. Long glimmering black hair, a pair of round dark eyes that can kill, and pouty red lips that beg to be kissed. To say we are inseparable the next few days is an exaggeration, but we enjoy ourselves in things like restaurants and the cinema. Spending time together we soon find out the one goes left where the other goes right, always a tight spot. We have nothing that really connects us besides the coincidence that the both of us are self-published authors, and how often do you run into one of those? She wrote a book about her failed relationship with a German pilot; the asshole was cheating on her, and I previously wrote a four hundred twenty-seven paged book in Dutch about the first thirty years of my life. How about that?

With my iron horse fully packed it takes less than half a day to arrive at the volcano of Cotopaxi. It stands at 19.347 feet in height and is clearly visible from afar. As it's actually active at the moment no one is allowed to go beyond the last refuge and all the way up. Not that anyone would be able to escape from the place where I hike up to when shit does hit the fan, but still. Visiting in winter has a downside because of the thick layer of grey clouds, preventing one from seeing the summit, that is hiding in there. Sharp winds are all around and I am out of luck when it begins to rain. Eyesight does not reach beyond twenty yards in this inclement bleakness where the absence of any form of life is disconcerting. Born and raised in the lowlands my heart is pounding in my chest, I am quickly out of breath and the altitude makes me dizzy. Human bodies are so sensitive and fragile. When rain increases, I go down and return in a rented jeep. My bike is not allowed into the park itself for nonsensical reasons, hence the car. For now I am fine with it since it is freaking cold anyway.

Pleasant smells of incense and a crispy fireplace wake me up in the morning. Corny yet calming sounds of pan flute music bring a smile to my sleepy face. Except for an alpaca in the garden, you know, one of those unchancy animals looking similar to a llama, it reminds me of a Swiss log cabin. Steamy meals with meat and vegetables, that the enclosed restaurant serve, are nothing less than excellent. Today the universe can't handle that I am dwelling in the purest of nature. While I am making an effort to escape the uselessness of things in western society, she is pulling my leg when my mate from back home texts me the leaked sex video's of a vile celebrity, performing oral sex and being urinated in the mouth. Just great. That gives another dimension to the word *leaked*.

On the moment of departure I change my destination because of new information provided by the owner of the hotel, which is a kind lady. This goes hand in hand with me being as impulsive as the mythological creature the Tyrannosaurus Rex. The pictures she shows me on her cellphone are convincing enough for me to head that way. Instead of directly going there I am sent in the wrong direction by my GPS, after a few good hours of driving. Having to endure more hours on horrible pine-covered mountain trails is the consequence. Thin air and steep loose sand paths have me going in the second gear only. At times, even in a challenging first. At one point I'm about to throw the navigation system, that had led me here, off of a large cliff. Standing right on the edge, it has a steep drop of about two hundred yards down. How can this device think this is the proper route? If I wouldn't have paid close attention and just blindly obeyed the navigation I would have plummeted towards my instant burial site. I am lost and fear I will not have enough gasoline to make it back. Nearby indigenous women tilling the ground in traditional clothing are surprised when I walk towards them to ask for directions. Not sure if it is the nerves of having a pale foreigner on their property or if it was their intent, for it soon proved itself, unfortunate as it is, they'd send me straight towards disaster.

Slowly descending on dry mud of an unknown track, I come to a sudden halt. Former landslides made half of the mountain collapse, now completely blocking the way. To my disadvantage, it is too steep to go back up. I am trapped in a very uncomfortable situation with a deep trench on one side and a dangerous cliff on the other. Adding to the malaise my bike has zero power in this thin air. It takes several attempts for the engine to give up and I am on the verge of doing the same. Just when I'm about to undertake the demoralizing act of getting all the luggage off to somehow push my way out of there I try one last thing. Which to my surprise actually works, albeit far from safely.

It is one of those moments in life where you are glad your mother isn't watching. Due to the steepness it is impossible to put my motorcycle on its standard. Everything I do I have to do while holding it with a firm grip. In a bouncing manner, I take position right angled toward the cliff as I try to level the ground with my boots. When I finally get the engine going I jump up, heading straight toward the edge in full throttle! This deep gaping hole being only a few yards in front of me I pull the handler ninety degrees at the right moment, with an almost impossible move, to prevent myself from plunging to my death! Zigzagging my way uphill goes so slowly that I could theoretically walk along. In doing so, gasoline is blasted out of my already almost empty tank. Despite the tempo, cold sweat is gushing down my back. Once on top, I stand there panting for breath, totally dehydrated. Even for my taste that was a little too close. Years later, while walking down a road or something, just being by myself, I can chuckle up when I think about these near-disasters, and I apprehend for a moment it is a miracle I am still alive.

Having my senses returned to me, I continue the ride with unknown directions. I reckon the smart thing to do is to go back the way I came from. Solely trusting my instinct now there are not many options left. It takes a while before stress levels drop and I finally spot that kid walking his alpaca, that I recognize from before, a pretty good reference point. With a lot of guesswork and paying close attention to anything familiar, I make it back to civilization on mere fumes of gasoline. Then a sigh of relief is released into the world.

Back on track, the cold turns trenchant. Green hills are making way for a more sinister chapter as they become rough pointy rocks. Of course, this is not uncommon on these altitudes in the middle of the Andes. It is a very scenic ride toward the destination, though getting harder to enjoy by the minute under these meagre conditions. I have admiration for the few folks I see, that are living in their primitive huts on the grassy slopes, removed from social well-being. Some sunshine would have made this so much more pleasurable. Instead, titans of clouds, haunted by gushes of wind, are getting darker and darker until they collapse under their own weight. By the time the hostel allows itself to be found nothing is dry anymore. Rain keeps slamming down all night from impenetrable clouds that have entangled my stay.

At almost four kilometers of altitude, the first daylight reveals what I came here for. Curious rays of sunlight perforating through the clouds make me stand in awe of a sight I didn't even know existed twenty-four hours ago. The extinct volcano of Quilotoa offers a massive crater, filled with a turquoise lake, which turns green depending on the light. Colored mountains that are protectively embracing the mystical waters make the scene perfect. Going to the foot of the lake on the sandy trail, you can choose to either walk down or take a horse or donkey for a few bucks. Around its shores, you can pitch your tent together with other utopians from a variety of nations, or rent a kayak. Hotels in the mini village at the top are ever helpful to provide information about the many hiking routes in the wide area, lasting from hours to several days. Craters and canyons are literally everywhere, remainders of a once so violent happening in the distant past.

On the way further south, I postpone my visit to a mountain I was planning to climb. The climbing gear I brought along makes my backpack significantly bigger than usual, hence I can't wait to check that one off the list so I can drop some of that gear for convenience sake, so far it doesn't exactly make the whole thing any lighter. By the time I reach the crossroads at Ambato the realization kicks in that my body had suffered a lot of cold weather lately. Time to change course.

As a result, my mind settles for the provincial town of Baños instead. I know I made the right choice when the sky starts turning blue along the way until it is fully clear. Feeling the mercury rising is pleasant. It's almost like taking some time off from traveling, going to this domestic vacation spot. Parallel to the winding roads lies a rushing river, the strong current is responsible for water splashing on the rocks, sticking out on the sides. These roads would certainly be fun to drive on if it wasn't for the insane winds I seldom experienced. Fierce squalls blow me toward the slopes repeatedly, forcing me to tightly grab my bike handles. In the midst of it all is a view on the snowy peak of the Tungurahua volcano; that scene is very promising. Adding to the beauty, a large mountain range across the valley has a blanket of intense white clouds crawling over the top, as if the heavens voluntarily try to get a hold of the mortal things below. Nearly entering town, it feels like a personal welcome to see huge bright letters on the rocks that read *Bienvenidos de Baños*.

This location certainly is inviting. Mainly known for its outdoor activities, it is also home of the nourishing thermal pools to help relax your tendons beneath affable waterfalls, flowing from pristine jungles in the hills. If you're interested in getting a professional back rub for unthinkably low prices, then this is the place to be, never deprive yourself of unknotting your muscles with such opportunities. Moreover, comprehensive lunches can be enjoyed at local restaurants for a few dollars. For dinner, there actually are sophisticated places with some fine cuisine on the menu. For the culinary daredevil there is grilled and deep-fried *Cuy*, as they call it, which is guinea pig. Now anything deep-fried usually tastes good, a leather shoe would probably suffice, yet from experience I can tell you that grilled guinea pig comes close to the taste of bad chicken. But hey, give it a try - you might think otherwise.

With a wide variety of outdoor sport facilities, the town is crammed with tour operators, they are over-the-top represented. Booking things like canopy tours or quad driving is easy. You will have a guaranteed adventure when repelling canyons and waterfalls, and more of that active stuff. Mind you, that certain waterfalls scattered throughout are worth visiting, being very high and beautiful such as the *Cascada de Chamada*. Opting for that perfect Instagram photo you can't afford to miss *La casa del árbol*, which, depending on the season, can be a bit touristy. It is basically a bunch of playground swings built on the edge of a ravine, which causes the illusion that you are flying. Overlooking a huge valley with a spectacular perspective of the near volcano, that now and again produces a gigantic plume of grayish smoke. Lame as it seems I have to admit the experience deserves some credit. And it's always cheap entertainment to watch other people get frightened by something as simple as a swing.

Along the way it is great to observe the beautiful faces of people, and analyze how they all look so similar over here, and so different from somewhere else. Autochthon women in bright-colored kirtles are roasting corn on small grids on the side of the road. Sometimes for private consumption, other times it is being sold. Driving through one lane villages I notice it is common for everyone to participate in collective interests, for instance, when a house needs to be built. From the corner of my eye I spot a middle-aged woman, fully ordained in traditional clothing, engaging in the activity of bar bending! This community spirit mentality fills my heart with joy.

Of course, I do need this country to get into the next, as is part of the pros and cons of traveling overland. However, the main reason for visiting Ecuador is my next destination, the erratic stratovolcano of Chimborazo. Dominating its brothers and sisters at well over six thousand meters, it is the highest extinct lava pit of the mountain range. It is often referred to as the Giant of the Andes. By the time I leave my retreat, my body is warmed up and my mind prepared for the climb, or so I think. Around Riobamba the weather takes a nasty turn that keeps getting worse as I go on. The heights cause me to move through clouds only. Not getting a lot of exercise while driving, the wetness cools my body down rapidly. Increasingly sharp winds are not exactly helping either. Not far from the entrance of the park, a dead horse lies next to the right lane. An agonized expression will be the last one on its face. It has lost the battle against the treacherous cold and I have to stay prudent to not be the next one in line. If it were not for my navigation, doing its job for a change, I surely would have passed the pearly gates. There is zero visibility in the declining obscuring weather. Uniformed guards sell me the same shit story as at Cotopaxi; I am not allowed any further on my motorcycle. Apparently, cars make less noise and do not chase away the wildlife. Sounds like a money-making scheme to me, thus hampering the rest of the day.

My hard headedness refuses to rent a jeep this time. In spite of persistent horrible weather, I start the long hike uphill after filling my stomach with bland lukewarm empanadas. To say I regret that decision is too much, but it is definitely one of the less amusing hikes I have ever had. Groups of alpacas don't look very happy either, and when alpacas are cold you know it is really cold. The dead horse near the entrance wasn't kidding. With a headache and out of breath I arrive at the *Carrel Refugio* after walking in the rain for hours, with the last hour in total darkness. My head torch acted as my only guide through these thick rainclouds, at a chilling four thousand eight hundred meters. In the wooden refuge I take off my leg gaiters and leave my wet clothes to dry. My walking sticks are content with the break as well, left to rest in the corner where they won't have to endure the pressure for a few more hours. Howling winds make the roof and walls creaky as the evening progresses, somewhat of a concerning sound. Outside on the snow-covered rocks, deposited for millennia without even a sliver of green; a reminder of the lifelessness at these altitudes where hardly anything survives.

The bad combination of hot chocolate and tuna filled wraps makes me nauseous all night. Together with lightheadedness, this is responsible for me not being able to sleep one second. Repeatedly I crawl out of my sleeping bag to try to throw up in the bathroom, which is freezing cold, tiny and entirely made out of wood. Whilst sitting on my knees my already empty stomach refuses to cooperate. I cannot prevent my condition from getting worse but for those that are familiar with Alpinism, you know that in the mountains you cannot act like a pussy. Far from being recovered, I gear up with the fading night to make my way to the last hut, *Refugio Whymper*.

Continuing upward, I pass the lake of *Laguna Condor cocha*, or what's left of it anyway. In this season the majestic lake has diminished to a mere puddle at five thousand one hundred meters. Soon after, the path disappears, making it more or less obvious why it is mandatory to hire a professional guide. Perhaps I should have done the same considering the horrible weather, instead of climbing solo which is highly illegal here. My stomach is still empty as I keep ascending in slow pace. My undiminished nausea is robbing me of the necessary energy. Also, dehydration is constantly lying in wait for me being so high up, my body needs more water than I can carry. By the time it is fully daylight several hours have gone by. Horizontally attacking snow and sleet blizzards are making it nearly impossible to continue. "I thought you could climb this one year around?" I am saying to myself. At least that is what I was told. Next time I better not listen to folks that have never done this before. Whatever you read online, it is hereby not recommended to climb Chimborazo in winter. I would love to head to the summit to conquer this grand baby, but have little choice other than returning to safety. Normally speaking, the way back should be much easier than going up. Apart from the fever, undoubtedly, bad physical preparation has its role in this too and makes it just as hard. Never underestimate the challenges of climbing; I know I brought this episode of ferment onto myself for not respecting the mountain enough.

Back at the entrance of the park I prepare to leave the snow behind me. However, the cold prevents my motorcycle to start properly as certain parts got covered in ice. Furthermore, the pouring rains aren't making it any easier. Once the engine is up and running it does not allow for shifting above the second gear for a good number of miles. Feelings of exasperation are in conclave with the cold and I can't feel my fingers anymore. Goggles are fogged up, preventing any form of visibility - oh the things one has to deal with sometimes. Little setbacks can become huge when everything is already working against you. Perhaps I should have chosen to spend my money more wisely by going to the tropical Galapagos Islands instead, as I know some other backpackers did. Yes, I can already see myself indulge in the heat. For now, I had really been gunning for this climb, and I accept my fate of having to let go of the attempt. Jesus said you can move mountains if you just believe. Well, I did exactly so. Namely moving it to another date in my agenda.

It almost takes me a week to recover. I am at that point in life where I need to start accepting I'm not in my early twenties anymore. Since the country is small I head back to Quito, where a fair accommodation helps me regain my strength. Feeling fit again and ready to hit the road, it takes four hundred twenty kilometers to drive to Guayaquil, an important city because it has one of the major South American ports. Going downhill for three and a half kilometers towards the coast is very satisfying. With the engine reclaiming full power, it is no longer an issue to throw it into sixth gear, absolutely consuming pavement. Warm and humid climates abound, this place is a jacket and a pants difference from where I was before, no need for thermo underwear. My spirit is lifted by the abundance of palm trees.

In the modern center, in front of the Continental hotel, rests the *Parque de las Iguanas*. It is something like an open air zoo without fences. The reptiles with long tails are in the trees and all over the well-maintained lawn, being lively green with sunshine. I have never seen so many iguana's together! Very amusing. Throughout the streets it's easy to find shops and restaurants, and there is plenty of art and music. A huge Ferris wheel, boasting on the shoreline of the *Malecon Simón Bolivar* promenade, romantically lights up at night. Not too far from here lies the district of Santa Ana & El Carmen with picturesque colored houses on a hill, stacked together like cubes. Another hill with an old white church and a lighthouse broadcasts a wide prospect across the river. A perfect place to stroll about and snap some photos.

At my mediocre hotel, an extroverted Venezuelan woman is determent to talk me into her room. Every day, we bump into each other in the hallway, where every time she begins to massage my shoulders and tries anything to be close. After seven days of rejection my body gives in and realizes (because it is the last night anyway) I am not only human but still a man with needs also. In her room, she starts kissing me right away and grabs for my, in the meantime, swollen manlyhood. Clasping it tightly in her hand, as if the situation wasn't weird enough, she yearns with her big eyes and says dead serious "I am looking for a life partner!" As a result I am too shocked to burst out into laughter. I think for a second and reply soberly, "Well that is one way of showing it!" To escape the awkwardness I lie that I'm not ready for such a commitment. In reality I am, just not with her. Don't you mind the pretty face; even if she'd lose forty pounds or so and becomes healthy, the pushy types are not very attractive.

I am more drawn to the ones with self-control. And what do you know? Later on while having a look in the city I meet a girl just like that. She happens to be from Venezuela also and is illegally in the country. Not that I care, she is a *mamacita* from head to toe. The night we spent is a wonderful memory to be cherished. Since she is on the rise to fame, I will not jeopardize her modeling career by mentioning her name, but seeing her more and more in newspapers and magazines, makes me think that she is doing okay.

Warm temperatures show no interest in the Guayaquil showers that keep coming down. The rays of the sun are intense. Factor 30 is the least level of sunscreen to use if you do not want to be grilled alive or alternatively, look like a scarecrow at the age of fifty. Wearing nothing but a shirt or thin jacket I have a bottle with me at all times. Resuming the big drive, not too far from the coast, I pass green rice patties on acceptable highways, that are more or less provincial roads in disguise. Once I reach harbor town Machala I am close to being deaf. For the last two hundred kilometers my messed-up exhaust pipe sounded like an air-raid alarm! Asking around in poor Spanish gets me to a mechanic shop within an hour. For as little as ten dollars I have it fixed the same day, ready while I wait.

While lingering in town for a few days it is relaxing to watch dull fisherman boats in the mangrove, where entire platoons of mosquitos are represented. Nonchalant barbers are shaving customers on sidewalks in the sunshine, canaries and parquets are chasing one another with a bright blue canvas in the background. Breakfasts consist of something that looks like a fat ball that you feed birds with in wintertime and it sure tastes as it looks. In evenings, I do not have to search for places to dine at all. On a lengthy street with broken curbs, the one towards the docks where most restaurants are located, it is so quiet that owners almost yank me inside. All watching each other closely, the competition seems as if it's a game here.

Another thing, not that I was paying attention to it, but I can't help noticing there are more people of color in this area. Because of this, every now and then the laid-back atmosphere is slightly disturbed by the gazing of somewhat intimidating groups of youth at this gringo, going about in their hood. My personality cannot resist staring right back in their eyes showing I am not afraid. Although that is probably one of the dumbest things one can do since they are all carrying weapons, carelessly showing them off. A positive result however, of this local ethnic mix, is that the ladies have less flat behinds like in the rest of the country. And being an ass-man myself, if you allow me to get graphic, I do appreciate those tight hot pants filled with nice bums.

Warm gentle winds are an encouragement once I start driving further. Once again, magnetic forces have my compass pointing south. Still being close to the equator, shadows are playing hide and seek with the sun directly overhead. At roadside stalls, the friendly people are selling freshly squeezed juice, produced from raw sugar cane. Available in substantial quantities, this healthy treat is always refreshing, not to mention delicious! For a moment I think about my times in Egypt, where I drank at least a liter and a half a day of that stuff. Fields of banana plantains are as far as the eye can see, similar to Moses going through the parted Red Sea on a narrow path, I find myself in between huge walls of green. Making my way through the lush maze it remains astonishing how empty the roads themselves are. On main arteries and in the cities it can be busy of course, yet in the rest of the country you wonder if you are the only one having survived the apocalypse. For the most part, I have both lanes to myself. How cool is that? When traffic does show up it's not holding me back either, driving in between cars, I pass everyone. On account of my bike being light in weight, I am the first one to go at sporadic traffic lights. My side mirrors reveal that the ones behind me are eating my dust.

Lost in thoughts I drift away to the countless hours wasted in traffic jams back home. So much valuable time thrown away in the useless, depressing, almost painful strings of immovable vehicles. All these moments spent standing still on highways with hundreds of thousands of people at once, every day again, is a reminder you are nothing but a slave to the system. A time, times, and half a time again, trapped in this iron ocean of crammed tension is something I cannot accept or somehow get used to. Standing still drives me nuts - no pun intended. With a piece of me dying due to the suffocating crowdedness, I feel compelled to eventually emigrate to a place with more space, in order to keep my sanity. Approaching the southeast border, I think to myself that I wouldn't mind ending up in this neck of the woods, so to speak. In spite of it all, without overstating it, I write in my journal that I enjoyed every single day of being in the excess of Ecuadorian beauty. I even learned to appreciate the inimitable sound of their hissing.

6

PERU

Grains of sand semblances the soft tarmac lanes; high temperatures and a poor subsurface are responsible for tracks of heavy freight transport; it has left outstretched hollows that are hard to drive on. During the summer season breezes are predominantly warm, even coming from the open ocean. Owning your own transport gives more independence one can wish for and being able to pretty much go wherever you want definitely is a great fortuity.

Arriving at the Peruvian border, I experience the lesser sides of it all when it takes four hours to cross. So much for my intention to drive a lot today. Six buses who beat me to the punch are spitting out a huge line of tourists. Finally having exited Ecuador and receiving a new stamp in my passport they tell me a certain paper is needed for my bike. To get this paper I must go back into Ecuador. So there I go, illegally into the country driving back eight miles. This illogical move is an omen for the rest of the travels with much more illogicalness to come. Upon my so-called second arrival, customs have just changed shifts. Now I have to explain it all again. If you could only see the look on their faces when they find out I am already officially in Peru. It is always a thrill when you enter a new country. Happy and excited to see something as simple as differently colored license plates on cars.

Torrid flats bring forth strong winds, so strong my drenched, rained-on clothes blow dry while driving. Winds get less strong as I approach the coastal village of Mancora, where pelicans bypass on the surface of the Pacific Ocean. Prehistoric looking seagulls in black tuxedos dominate the beaches, making crabs crawl back into their diligently dug out holes. On crumbly street corners in the town's cozy center dodgy figures offer marihuana and cocaine. A funky barbershop refurbishes my worn-out hair and stunted facial hair for a reasonable price. My goodness, those transgenders of today know how to give a haircut. To maintain those typical southern vibes of the late seventies I only leave my mustache. In a hostel, right on the beach I run into some travelers I previously met. At this place, the food is good and cheap enough to make me linger for a while. In two days time I eat more than in the previous two weeks combined. One thing is certain, never before did I listen to so much German rap music. Provided by the insane amount of young German volunteers everywhere. They are represented in such a way it makes you wonder if they are secretly planning the next worldwide invasion!

One might think I am doing it on purpose, but when I enter the chaotic and polluted city of Chiclayo I accidentally check-in into another one of those clandestine whorehouse hotels. By now, I am not too convinced myself either. On a serious note though, it is disconcerting to come across so much prostitution everywhere I go. Imagine the things I do not come across. Checking out the pictures of the girls on the laminated brochure makes my heart sad. What a life eh? A warm shower washes off the dust and mud from dirty desert roads.

I can promise goodbye to my planned visit to the ruins of

Cajamarca. Floods due to incessant rains are putting a spanner to it around Piura. Many roads are blocked or completely submerged. One of the main routes holds a moist surprise in store, because there is no other way I need to cross forty meters of muddy water. Driving through a foot-deep mud bath I pass hundreds of stationary cars and trucks, and because of the road block they are profusely honking their horns. One by one, they take the chance to cross. Semi-trucks and buses are doing alright but several cars get stuck right away as murkiness drowns their engines, it being deeper towards the middle section. It also fills up the interior as presumptuous idiots left their windows rolled down, letting the smudge flow right through. Bystanders are paying close attention when it is my turn, joining me in expecting the worst. With my boots tied on the back and without socks, I go all out in first gear. I get stuck when rubbish in the thick water makes the stretched chain come off. Luckily two of those bystanders give me a helping hand and push me ashore. On dry land, that same helping hand needs to be filled with coins, which I do gladly. They even put the chain back on, surrounded by the sounds of spurting and failing engines, which must have lasted for weeks. I am wet up to my knees and look like a pig but I made it.

Mud still stuck under my toenails I continue my route to the outskirts of Trujillo. Along the way, the roadsides are covered in litter and plastic. My oh my, what a garbage dump. The waste that remote tiny villages are producing is scattered across the sandy plains by strong winds. Approaching the center, car drivers have a special trick they like to use in busy traffic. Instead of using a signal, drivers will often just stick their arm out of the window. This action apparently gives them the right to do whatever the hell they want. I begin to think people are born with a defect which makes them unable to yield. Ever.

Strolling around the square in the center and through the anything but boring shopping streets of the old city, makes up for it all. At night romantically lit-up colonial buildings are pleasant to the eye and there are restaurants with local dishes, plenty of sightseeing and culturally laden activities. Still some folks manage to interrupt this laid-back city. Namely, angry social justice warriors are holding a march for women's rights. Armed with banners and bullhorns they subjugate the population to note their demands. But then again, contrary to those millennial suck-ups in the West, they might actually have a valid point here.

Whereas many tourists exclusively roll in for Peru's main attraction, that will be addressed later on, the archeological site of Chan Chan is widely neglected. Therefore, not getting the attention it deserves in my opinion. This ancient harbor city was big enough to house ten thousands of people, perhaps more. A huge blueprint is unfolding as I explore the perimeter. What did they need five-meter high walls for? Hundreds of meters long and a meter thick this is a hefty fortress. Animal figure stone cuttings, multiple inner courts the size of four soccer fields and geometrical mysteries. A wet dream for any amateur archeologist such as myself. Spread out all over the place only a hand full of visitors roam around. Surely, they won't notice if I pass a few restricted areas would they? No major discoveries but so worth to feel the rush of spying shielded terrain. Checking if no one is watching I spot two white orbs hovering in the clear blue sky. Now I will never be an advocate for alien grey's, that is not what I am saying, but these things are by definition Unidentified Flying Objects. I walk over to three tourists carrying *Nikon's* with those differential lenses, of which you would guess they could zoom in on the smallest moon crater. They are quite baffled upon the sight of these white orbs yet seem less intrigued than I am. How can anyone not be? Not too long ago in Colombia I saw two flying black pyramids. Once again, I am not claiming to have a thing for UFOs or something and I was not using drugs. At least not at that particular time. To my limited knowledge, they remain unidentified.

A well-performing engine sends me to an uncompromising strip, pointing all the way to the horizon via Chimbote. Here stands one of the highest sand dunes I have ever seen. Creative mountains about so elegantly mingle red, brown and khaki. Arriving in the miniature village of La Gramita my plan to spend the night here fails. The few places they usually have are rented out due to a big wedding feast. So much for relaxing on the beach in a romantic bay. Now I'm forced to come up with a backup plan that I was too tired for to make earlier on. A local residence happens to be able to fill up my gas tank and jerry can and with that potential issue tackled I am on the move again. Harsh and probing faces of the townspeople rhetorically bid me farewell. Now I am able to cross parched and unknown levels without gas stations for dozens of miles.

A single night is spent in the snooze-fest town of Huarmey. Among other provinces, this town is struck by heavy floods and rainfall. In the meantime, six hundred and forty thousand people are affected. A serious disaster! No drinking water, no food and many of them have lost their houses. On the news the word is out that certain mayors were bribed on a massive scale to grant houses being built on dried up riverbeds. Unfortunately, when the rain came the old rivers remembered how they used to flow and deposited all their water that way. Ever biased international media platforms hardly cover the incredible devastation. So far, Colombia is the only other country that sends money and aid.

Villages sticking out by their unorganized filth and more deserts take me to an advantageous coastal route, cut out through sharp rocks. Billows of perfect blue water smile with the flickering of the sun. Sand of large dunes are light enough to hurt one's eyes when not fully protected. Such a contrast, it seems a different world when moments later I hit the capital's suburbs. To say it's a big mess wouldn't do it justice, yet of course it is to be expected with a city counting nine million heads. A polluted labyrinth of chaotic traffic and danger all around. Divided into forty-two districts, of which about six are nice and the rest are unsafe and full of tumultuous mayhem. Even though I am very tired I arrive unscathed, almost miraculously, in downtown Lima.

What a mentality. At a garage to get my motorcycle fixed, I have to keep the keys in my pocket. According to someone who is helping me getting around, the mechanic would otherwise drive away and steal it! You cannot find potato chips anywhere and streets are filled with casinos, that apparently go hand in hand with deserts, and perhaps with Indian looking types of people. City buses have their destinations handwritten on the sides, and the smell of the tap water is a strong indicator not to drink from it, for all I know it might actually be one hundred percent chlorine. Furthermore, certain streets, filled with unending rows of the exact same shops, are loaded with things like hospital beds and brand-new dentist-chairs. How can any business survive, exclusively selling these items?

Not one negative word though, if you cannot enjoy the wealthier touristy districts you might want to look in the mirror. At least in the summer season, I admit the winters are tedious and grey. Starting with Miraflores, being the place to be for exclusive restaurants and luxurious shopping malls. Of course, the Park of Love is where you want to take your lover to see amorous sunsets across the ocean, which is done every night by couples in love. Surfing at that same beautiful coastline can be done on good waves when the tide rolls in. Downtown has indoor markets, such as the famous Inca Market, where they sell clothes and carpets made of alpaca wool, with archeological sites rising out between modern buildings. Here and in San Miguel very interesting pre-Inca culture pyramids can be found, for instance at *Huaca Huallamarca* and *Huaca Pucllana*. A must see if you are around.

In Barranco you will stumble upon artistic graffiti-covered walls in narrow stairways, making the pale concrete more charming. Local students come here daily to make photographs and portraits. Other prominences are satisfying musicians, cozy coffee corners, marihuana smoking hippies, the best ice cream in town and vegan restaurants, where you should not expect a drink to be served before your meal arrives. Streets are filled with overweight people. By observation one of the reasons might be the fact that every lunchroom has a bottle of Inca Kola on the table. Peruvians easily empty a bottle a day of the yellow sugary good that has at least twice the amount of sweeteners as the darker version of the Coca Cola Company.

Over the course of days, a chicken arepa makes me so sick that I am emptying my chime in the loo all night. But where's the fun if you don't try to eat things you never had before? Contrary to my own interests, if you consider yourself a salsa enthusiast I know just the place. It is not entirely without the danger of being mugged, but Callau is where it all began according to oral traditions. In the area known for its graffiti art it is also recommended not to roam streets by yourself if you value your life. The grandfathers of salsa as well as other progressive artists in the scene are painted on facades of houses and shops. They are serious about this heritage, when bringing up the subject, locals can talk for hours on end. Once you made it here and managed to stay alive you might as well visit the hotspots of much safer areas. For example, the ghost-haunted castle *Castillo de Chancay*, a well-preserved submarine at the harbor, or the docks where the Spaniards loaded all the stolen gold on their decks, with mild renovations the docks still being intact today. Another thing that won't go unnoticed, is that everywhere around, from supermarkets to restaurants - including the fancy one's, the cashiers thoroughly inspect your paper money as if you have serious intentions to scam them! Although they do it to everyone else, I can't help feeling a little embarrassed.

In the big city, I arrange an expensive hotel for a special occasion, with the biggest bed I have ever seen. As a surprise, my Colombian fling from two chapters ago is boarding up for a week. Yes, this Latina means business. No issue to hop on a plane for a visit. We stroll along the beaches and cruise on boulevards with well-kept lawns, brightened up by a red and white painted lighthouse. To celebrate her birthday we end up in an upscale restaurant, the glamorous *La Rosa Nautica*, where it's not surprising to dine next to celebrities. Incoming waves are robustly pounding against the poles that defy the wooden establishment, built right on the coast. At the edge of the district of Chorrillos, a big white statue of Jesus Christ is watching out over the city from a hill. On that same hill she decides to give me a blowjob in broad daylight, where I reckon it impossible for others not to have seen this. I guess I always had a thing for the crazy ones.

Due to nationwide floods, Lima also is bedeviled with no warm water from the showers. Soon enough this turns into no water at all. You can even forget about flushing the toilet. Residents harboring all bottled water leaves supermarket aisles empty. Things seem to be going from bad to worse until it appears the fun just started.

On the very day the cute attorney heads home, I check out of the hotel and into a hostel I hadn't been before. Upon arrival, I have an instant click with the girl from the reception, who coincidentally is having her first day on the job. Little did I know this motivated individual is just months away from opening her own hostel. She hardly stands five feet tall and assures me good things come in small packages. Well, I am not going to get into details here but let's just say she was not lying. Her eyes ensnare like a Taiwanese street girl, and awkwardly I mean that in a complementary way. As time passes, she lets me know that every full moon causes a merging of souls with a deep connection due to her incredible Inca powers. There is definitely a magnetic force at work here, for instance, we dance the night away in aromas of sweat and cheap beer on the Latin version of Oktoberfest, and ride bicycles along the palm trees of the chivalrous boulevard during sunsets. Before I can fully grasp the fleetness of things, holding true to the Latin traditions, I get introduced to her parents as well as other family members. Thus, even agreeing to attend a traditional wedding ceremony of a step-sibling, where we make fun of those that had one too many.

Due to an upcoming expiring passport, I order a new one at the Dutch embassy in Lima, which is not surprisingly located on the thirteenth floor of a slick office building. Hiding in plain sight, a quote from Pythagoras comes to mind: "All things are number." Undoubtedly the new document will take a few weeks before it is ready. Seeking activities to kill the time I meet up with two men that have quite the story to tell.

Of the last fifteen months of their lives they'd spent seven and a half of those in jail! And not just any jail but the notorious *Castro Castro* on the outskirts of Lima. For a while home of Dutch criminal Joran van der Sloot who obtained a certain level of fame by killing American national Natalee Holloway, never revealing where he dumped the body except for vague clues he gave on a hidden camera, secretly being recorded. Later he was responsible for ending the life of a Peruvian girl in a hotel room, for which he is doing time now because he got sloppy, even though no one knows her name. The gentlemen I now meet shared the same lawyer, until he lost faith in Joran and quit defending him. This is the extraordinary story of Dustin Kent, an American sports car loving nurse from California who was falsely accused by his Peruvian ex-wife for kidnapping his own daughter. This in collaboration with a former commando of the British Army, who later worked as a bodyguard to the English football team, the ever-charming mister Kevin Critchley. According to British newspaper *The Telegraph* last named was hired to, and I quote, take the five-year-old girl back from the mother in this custody battle, end quote. Speaking about killing the time - as they share their story it turns out they have been drinking quite a bit, if not being chronically besotted, as a way of not having to deal with the atrocities they witnessed behind bars. Who can blame them? Not to mention Kevin had to miss the birth of one of his children. Extensive televised news coverages have given them a certain celebrity status in Peru. Unfortunately, more like in a notorious way, resulting in some sort of a witch hunt. They actually get kicked out of a few hotels when the owner recognizes them. Getting to know each other, we come up with the bold step to return to prison, with all the conceivable repercussions.

As former inmates the chance of getting back in is almost guaranteed. For me however, we have to figure out a way to sneak me in. The only chance the heavily guarded *Castro Castro* offers is on Sunday, which is male visiting day, solely accessible for relatives. Not backing down now, a masterplan is forged after a few classified phone calls with contacts within the walls. I can barely contain my excitement until the day has come, the unforgettable day where I am rebranded as the cousin of a highly sinister Romanian drug lord. Do not mind me, I'm just strolling along to visit my uncle, who so happens to be half Dutch. How epic is that? You can't make this stuff up.

Upon arrival, we have to walk the last bit towards the doomful complex, on account of our taxi driver bailing out. Getting all nervous he rather avoids this place and rightly so, being in a neighborhood that feels far from safe, with unpaved streets. Moreover, the graffiti-covered reinforced concrete walls with barbed wire, the hostile overshadowing watchtowers, and all the gates with uncountable steel bars, do not come across as a place you would voluntarily visit. Yet here we are. After a firm examination by the numerous prison guards, we are let in. Our arms are varnished in hard to erase stamps and we get marked with several numbers with those black permanent markers. It is as if we are being detained in a hidden away Second

World War gulag or something. One guard started whining about our shoes and wants to send us back; laces can cause for all kinds of trouble. One of my companions knows how to play this game and gives him some cash, easing the situation. Being fenced in all day and behind bars is an experience I did not have for years. Back in the days, I worked in several Dutch prisons for a few years, including the infamous *Bijlmerbajes*. Being pushed along iron barriers like cattle I suddenly find myself surrounded by various nationalities of criminals, most of them being hard cases. Thieves, rapists, drug traffickers, pedophiles and even cold-blooded murderers. Going about, some inmates are urged by others to pull up their shirts and show the scars of bullet holes and knife attacks. With knife attacks I mean they were literally sliced open, absolutely brutal. I can hardly believe my eyes. Mexicans show off their *zippers*, which is jargon for the scars on one's tummy for operatively inserting bags of drugs. An intimidating seven feet tall buff from Serbia complains about the kilo prices of cocaine in Amsterdam.

Within five minutes, I get offered liquor, illegally brewed in the consecutive compound. I learn the ins and outs of how to bribe the guards who are smuggling it into this one. Not a drinker myself but curious as always I take a tiny sip to see what they are so excited about. I cannot say it taste any different than turpentine smells. If that is not wicked enough, the gym is transformed into a gambling joint and if you want to be tattooed - *no problemos*.

Spending time with several inmates, I get the chance to be locked up in one of the actual cells. You know, to get the ultimate feeling of how awful that might be. With the steel door closed, I get an impression of how small and uneasy the inside really is. To my surprise, within ten seconds, I am offered cocaine. Initially not a fan of the drug but this is a chance I cannot afford to miss. Diving my face into the so-called Nazca lines, I take two big hits. Snorting coke in a Peruvian jail cell. Check! Yep, been there done that. It is so strong that I cannot feel my palate anymore. It even gets worrisome when half of my skull turns numb, but I feel fantastic! For the rest of the day I walk with my head in the clouds.

For obvious reasons, there is no shortage of Dutch guys in this prison. All independently in for the same thing – drug smuggling. One of them was a successful businessman operating in transport. He thought he would make a quick buck by filling up the asparagus cans with something else. When that plan backfired he had to do several decades. Another one had a bunch of casinos all over Europe as a cover for his, let's say, ancillary services. Due to misbehavior, another guy resides in *the hole*, as they nicknamed solitary confinement. Yet another, also having a green thumb, was not building up enough pension as a plumber, resulting in wasting half of his life away in bumfuck nowhere. They are actually pleased to meet a fellow kinsman. Being introduced to certain people, the wildest stories start to surface.

Another freak whacked his visiting prostitute and had her bricked-in in his own cell. He cunningly tried to hide her under the constructed bed until body fluids came creeping out. To make the crew complete, it is also the home of a former American citizen that became famous as the suitcase murderer, because that's where he put his girlfriend in after he had chopped her up. Pretty gruesome. Things suddenly get real when I find out that someone who according to the official story escaped, lies six feet under instead, not too far from the complex. Now that is one successful cover-up. Last but not least, there is an ill-looking Welsh man, who had an unfortunate encounter with Customs on his sailing yacht, hiding a ridiculous amount of kilo's below deck. He is not too happy with his additional seven years over an already long sentence. You better not get caught with a cellphone, although it is something almost everyone has. Of course, I cannot tell you the how and where but boy are they clever with hiding those things. But to give you one example of how inventive they are; one of the Mexicans shows me how he cut a bar of soap in half, having diligently scooped out the inside of both parts creating a hollow space, thus having a place to put a tiny cellphone. Closing the two parts together with some water or saliva around its edges, it is as nothing ever happened and fully undetectable. Compared to this *The Shawshank Redemption* and *Escape from Alcatraz* are child's play. Not that I had something as crazy as this in mind when I left home, but this surely is traveling to the core. It feels somewhat as a relief to exit the building at the end of the day without any uphold. Trying my best to keep my eyes and jaw steady as we pass the guards on the way out, for I am still high as a weather balloon.

My fully equipped motorcycle is shining in the early morning hours. Before moving on and bringing a closure to the madness in Lima, here are two anecdotes of what happened on later visits to this massive city. On my most recent one, you can say that I was at the right place at the right time. Namely, I had the honor of witnessing Keiko Fujimori being brought straight to jail with loud sirens of a wild police escorted convoy, rushing through the city's maze as in a movie, the press on their tail with a cameraman hanging out from a vehicle with sixty kilometers per hour. For those less involved in political matters, Keiko, being the opposition leader and daughter of the disgraced ex-president Alberto, is now being accused for alleged money laundering on a large scale, including the scandal of the Brazilian construction giant Odebrecht, involving many more South American politicians, which came to the surface about a year prior to this downfall.

As if all that wasn't enough already, I end up in the next unforeseeable event concerning high-status people. Walking into the airport, a couple just walks out, and not the least of one. Ah, I learn that I'm not the only one that has recognized them. Soon enough, they are awaited by a sea of cameras from the media and enthusiasts, when this country is graced by a royal visit from King Felipe the 6th, and his queen Letizia, the monarchs of Spain. Isn't it interesting, the things you can encounter when forsaking your television set for a moment and choose to go backpacking instead.

Coming back to the story at hand, with good headwind it takes half a day's journey to relocate to the harbor town of Paracas. Here shorelines are loaded with fishing boats, some boats bobbing close to the beach are entirely covered with pelicans. An old man walks barefoot in the sand, wearing a marine captain's hat with a little gold anchor on the front. Carrying a tin bucket in his hand, he is feeding leftovers of fish to the pelicans who are ravenous, but so used to the man that they are at a distance of only a few feet. Impatient seagulls don't stand a chance against the vigorous beaks snatching everything away.

This town has a derisory museum that displays one of world's greatest and best kept secrets in history. It is my sole purpose for being here, and what a delight to see something with your own eyes that is a regular on your bucket list. Widely covered on shows such as History Channel's *Ancient Aliens* are the renowned elongated skulls, now proven by scientists to be not human. I feel like hitting the end of a rainbow. Overjoyed, I spend hours in a room that is so small in size you could literally see everything in thirty seconds. Deceiving plaques in the glass display cabinets describe the anomalies of the skulls as mere cranial deformations, however, any rational and unbiased mind knows that is simple impossible.

For those less obsessed concerning the matter one can also book a fairly inexpensive boat tour to the nearby islands of *Las Ballistas* to spot sea lions. It is guaranteed they will be there. Despising boats myself, I soon find there is plenty of other stuff to undertake. Towards the peninsula are colonies of pink flamingos, residing there year around. A small nearby museum is worth the visit if antediluvian cultures spark your interest. Burial rituals, crockery with painted and inscribed strange-looking creatures, and more elongated skulls. Needless to say

I'm not passing this one. Close-by is a sediment of rock that holds shell fossils. According to the sign, I am looking at something that is thirty-six million years old. I cannot imagine why anyone would actually believe that. Especially since the Geological Column was literally grabbed out of thin air, and carbon dating is proven one hundred per cent unreliable. Or, as we like to say in the Netherlands: 'wet finger work'.

Deeper into the unapproachable lies *Playa Roja*, which owes its name to a red beach. Sandy hills and desert plains mixed with salt are in contrast with the supreme blue sky. Definitely an amazing thing to see, such serenity and completeness. The dryness of the air makes visibility beyond crystal clear. Opposite the turquoise bay from the viewpoint *Lagunillas* I spot a group of dolphins - just like that in their natural habitat! And all I had to do was come here. I'm tempted to join them in the refreshing waters. Ocean winds make the scorching heat bearable; they do not hamper the experience at all.

Something least expected to find in this climate are penguins, yet they fill up brown boulders in the breakers. They keep me entertained as my belly enjoys an overpriced fish at the only restaurant for miles around. Aromas of a grill always know how to persuade my appetite - effortlessly. An obese waiter in a stained button shirt serves me a chicha morada, a delicious national sweet drink made from burgundy corn cobs. Continuing on a salt path to beautiful rock formations, not far from Playa Raspon, I find remote hidden beaches, unaware to the general public. Several deep caves, seemingly unexplored, make this an emerald of a spot. Jealous crabs are fighting each other while others are skillfully digging holes in the white sand. Fun fact about the roads is that they appear to be worn out pavement. On further inspection they are proven to be pure salt, grayish in complexion because it is pressed by foot soles and tires. Money is well spent coming here to the salt deserts with ginormous sand dunes, manifestly belonging to the natural gems of this world.

Another town hosting elongated skulls is Ica. In their museum it is illegal to take photographs for obvious reasons once inside. They strictly watch every move as I hand over my camera and bag. What they are not paying attention to is how my cellphone is still in my shorts' pocket. Scowling security cameras on the ceiling cannot prevent me from snapping a few shots of the infamous mummified corps, alongside pottery with images of humanoids and hybrid animals, far from mythical creatures. Having gathered new material to make my case against our hidden origins I travel for fifteen minutes to the main attraction.

There are hordes of people racing toward this tiny desert town, the nearby oasis of Huacachina. Towering sand dunes, clutches of palm trees and a lake that I highly recommend not to swim in if you do not want to get sick. You can actually see white worms floating in the shallow water! The formerly astounding place of tranquility is ruined as tourism has absolutely raped it. Far less romantic than the promising brochure pictures. However, once you are there anyway you might as well enjoy the adventurous outdoor activities everyone is here for in the first place. I never knew that sliding off three hundred feet high dunes is so addictive. Sand boarding on the smooth surface is a lot of fun, with speeds that get your adrenaline going for sure! Buggy drivers crossing groups of thrill-seekers around seem to have a death wish. They steer straight toward edges and perform some pretty dangerous maneuvers. Sounds of loud engines fill the beautiful Ica desert, that somewhat kidnaps the innocence it was once clothed with. Placed in the front seat large sums of grit blow straight in my face. Gnashing my teeth it goes everywhere and even fills up my socks and underwear. Caressing the purest of sands, delicate winds create all kinds of wavy contours. Staying in the desert as the last group, we partake in the thrilling activity until sundown. On top of one of the largest dunes around, we revel at the marvelous sight of the orange glow. Driving back in the dark is action bound.

Evenings are spent in restaurants with other backpackers. Some also facilitate an area where you can dance. To watch these tipsy white guys trying to flirt with the ladies is absolutely cringeworthy, their stone hips not able to move to the sexual styles of Latin music. Tables are filled with fish-based dishes and a jumble of seafood, more often than not accompanied by the spicy substance of *ceviche*. Not missing on any table for that matter, nation's pride and joy, the unequivocally alcoholic drink of Pisco sour, basically being a wine brandy.

Through the vast and outstretched places my free education of the world continues. Harsh winds never seem to cease on this unending plain where the horizon constantly keeps moving backwards. However, you won't hear me complain too much as anything is better than rain. Extra gasoline is brought along to prevent a deja vu from my ten-thousand-kilometer-long trip on a motorcycle through Asia. I am not planning on getting stranded for days this time! Huge tracks of land have some small tornados forming as columns of sand sway through the air like a ballerina. In the afternoon, I get rewarded for my share of hardships as I arrive at a location that in my mind is unfathomable for it not to be fascinating. Having pulled over, excitement levels rise when I climb up the stairs of a strategically placed watchtower and encounter my dream converse into reality. Ancient mysterious figures of unknown origin drawn in dry lands by neatly sweeping the top layer aside, the substrate being a hue lighter. The first one can be seen right from the road! Of course, there are theories of which pre-Inca culture possibly could have made them, but that is all they are and ever will be: theories. What a graceful experience to drive a brand new motorcycle for thousands of kilometers, now finally alongside signatures of the gods, the much-publicized but little known of Nazca Lines.

The following day a diminutive dose of patience is needed. Due to the Easter weekend, it is busier than usual at the local domestic airport. When the moment is finally there, I position myself in the small one engine airplane, a little too small for my comfort. But nothing ventured nothing gained right? As soon as we are airborne nerves fade away. At last, I can enjoy the incredible moment of seeing the Nazca Lines and figures from the sky. Or can I? As a way of preparation, I postponed breakfast for after the flight. When the sudden movements begin I have just enough time to see two geoglyphs before I throw up in a plastic bag. We go from left to right in insane angles to fly around the animal figures for the best possible view. My dizziness is so intense that I can only keep my eyes closed. My balance disorder kicks in hard, firmly pressing my eyelids together is the only thing preventing me from continually throwing up. Of course, a hyperventilation attack can't lack when you should be having the time of your life. My back gets all damp and sweat is pouring down my stuffy face, still buried in the plastic bag. While heavily panting the copilot informs through my headphone we are right above the spider, and moments later at the monkey. I am so sick I cannot see shit and miss the whole damn thing. How ironic is that? I have undergone famines and wars to get here and all I get to see from the sky is the bottom of a condensing bag with vomit. Back at the airport, the promise is made to never ever board such a godforsaken cunt of an airplane again! It leaves me sick all day and nauseous up to two days after. Never again.

From here to Cusco it is about six hundred and seventy five kilometers. Other than a few brief moments, this way consists entirely out of winding mountain roads. It all runs smoothly in the beginning of this two-day trip. Two days and one night I should say. Rapidly gaining altitude makes the view splendid when starting out and I can see five times further than the mathematical equation of earth's curvature should allow me to see. That certainly makes me wonder, I just can't wrap my head around that. Dry brown rocks steadily change into a green wonderland that I formerly only knew from the Alps and the Caucasian Range. However, this is the Andes, and she has a trick up her sleeve.

When the first drops fall from the sky I wish I knew where my rain pants are hiding, not in my bags anyway. Black clouds are low enough to veil mountaintops, throwing down thunder and lightning, landslides and falling rocks force you to be aware and alert at all times; this is not to be taken lightly and in fact extremely dangerous. When rains greatly increase, I start shivering from the cold. Once above four thousand meters a hailstorm is torturing my hands and face. My fogged-up goggles compel to lower them so I can peek over and actually see where I am going. Soaked until my underwear a windowless shack appears in a field next to a frosty lake. On the side of the shack, a crappy awning saves the day. Just big enough to cover my motorcycle and me.

Prolonged hail turns everything white. Attempts to stay warm by jumping around are in vain and growing icicles on the front of the awning tell me it's time to get changed. I start unpacking my luggage with stiffened fingers in search of dry clothes. However, will they prevent further chance of hypothermia? My teeth are chattering continuously by now. I am out of supplies and will have to endure an empty stomach, which will only further stimulate my negative thoughts. Ice water dripping from the roof fills up a bottle that's good for drinking. As the night starts conquering the day, I force the lock of the door to broaden my options. It seems like I will be spending some time here. Inside the shack I find a useless dirty table and also a wheelbarrow, that, when put down on its handle bars, forms a seat. Having placed some clothing and a towel on my fabricated lounge chair, I am prevented from freezing to the icy cold iron. When darkness is all around the puddles and mud freezes rock solid. All I can do to kill the time is trying to catch some sleep. However, the increasing cold has no intention to allow it. At one point my muscles tense up in an irreversible way. I get so cold that moving along becomes a serious option.

Around one after midnight the clouds break open, seeing my chance to escape, when my worst nightmare becomes reality. My motorcycle will not start! Several failed tries have left the engine dead, perhaps flooded, just what I need. Now I have to wait for the sun to warm it up. But in the likely event the bad weather returns I am screwed anyway. Around four in the morning, I cannot handle the boredom any longer. The sleepless night motivates me to give it another shot. While temperatures remain the same, I get the engine going at a certain moment. My prayers have been answered. For about ten minutes, I have to give extra gas for the weak engine to keep on running. Meanwhile clouds have almost disappeared revealing uncountable stars. Looking up, the befuddling voluminous night sky turns to high definition, the Great Rift is clearly visible.

When I start driving, my body cramps in no time. As I go, I can feel my knees freeze solid. Sharp winds laugh at me as they pierce the scarf protecting my face, and continue to mock my gloves that seem like paper tissue, thus torturing my finger joints. It probably isn't a shocker when I tell you the Andes is a little short of streetlights. Hours and hours pass in thick darkness but every once in a while a semi-truck with blinding headlights breaks through, disorientating me. In the deadly aloneness all my bets are placed on a liberating sunrise to warm up the atmosphere. Forget it, none of that is here. At dawn, it becomes clear the army of clouds have reappeared. Layers of mist makes everything very moist. On account of the altitude and lack of water, I am thirsty and have a pounding headache. I had no food since yesterday's breakfast. Am I hungry? You betcha! At one point I have to pull over to step off for aid. Despite not being able to feel my feet and fingers, I was still experiencing excruciating agony. Rubbing them until they defrost is a painful process, and surely I would be better off without my runny nose. I find out the hard way that I am seriously underdressed for these conditions, but apart from yesterday's wet outfit I am already wearing all I have! Peeking about, I notice this area is overrun by fields of alpacas. For the first time I do not see them grazing on their own as they usually do. Now they all cling together in large groups to stay warm. Three dead cows had wished for an extra layer over their biological leather jacket. I am in so much pain that I begin to desire to lay on the ground. With my last bit of sanity I know this is not beneficial to do now, so I gather the little energy I still possess, and keep on driving with an empty tank, adding to the level of stress. Because stranding here in between the hills, where hardly any other traffic passes, is a guarantee to a certain death.

Solely on fumes, I actually make it to the first gas station at the edge of a small one-street village. This place is good for a local breakfast. A disgusting substance, but *they* seem to enjoy the dish with rotten potatoes. It is a process in which the vegetables get frozen and defrosted to create a certain taste. Sitting at a table in the tavern with my jacket still on, aimlessly staring in front of me, I notice the reflecting windows reveal a horrible face. One that got twenty years older in just one night. God, I look awful. Almost too exhausted to drive, I continue my trip with a deep breath and squinted eyes. Around five in the afternoon, the red-bricked city of Cusco reveals itself. I can't believe I made it. Only a check-in and a quick shower are standing in the way of me and my bed, where barely an hour later, I fall sound asleep.

Tensions between the various tribes for decades in Peru's jungles have driven an increasing number of people to the city and for that reason, it has grown exponentially. So much so, that the airport is walled in by new residential districts. If you live there you can literally wave to the pilots in the cockpit from your balcony - that's not good. Shops around *Plaza de Arba* in the vivacious center as well as shops in neighboring streets sport stockpiles of colorful blankets and sweaters of alpaca wool. I am advised to not accidentally mix it up with llama wool. Although a lot cheaper, saleswomen tell me it itches like hell. Walkways and squares are flooded with girls begging to give massages. Most tourists make the mistake of ignoring those deals. Massages are super cheap and the techniques are both professional and up to date. Seems like a win-win situation to me. At the immigration office, the government official stamps my newly begotten passport, enabling me to eventually bridge borders without problems. This might surprise you, but I actually like doing things the legal way. As in any other South American country, paperwork takes up half the day. They send me to the bank for authorization of a payment, to the store to make copies of a bunch of things, and the list of errands goes on and on.

Mind you, that nothing can break my spirits today. Fascinated by the next archeological site for at least a decade you can imagine that it is quite the thrill going there. Being able to hike up I can overlook the city of Cusco from the hill where the sun rises. How amazing to walk among the humongous hewn stone blocks that fit so tight that no mortar is needed. Nowhere in the long walls can you even put something as thin as razorblades in the joints. Of course, I am talking about the legendary *Saqsayhuaman*, which when pronounced sounds a bit like a retarded person saying sexy woman. Shrouded in mystery the blocks weighing multiple tons have left mainstream archeology baffled. Picking up some of what guides from passing tour groups are saying, it seems they are just making wild guesses, filling in the blanks of history as it were. As one quarry and the stones themselves clearly suggests, the building material had to be soft during construction of the immense structure. Perhaps even close to liquefied.

Driving around on my motorbike, I get the chance to visit many points of interest. Thus a comparative case goes for the century-old city of *Chinchero*. There are less huge blocks but both sites share more or less the same architecture. Anyone can see where the ancients left off and from where the Incas picked up with totally different styles, the lower layers being first and older, and much more sophisticated. Who knows if the original version was destroyed by a flood filling up the enclosure? I am just throwing it out there. Atlantis-like structures inspired by constellations with geometrical measurements aside, today it has an adjacent village with bumpy rocky roads. Walking up the slope I watch these same roads, compiled from stones with machine grind joints that prevent sliding when it gets slippery. Women dressed in local robes have their hair ordained in long braids. The men, sitting on wicker stools, carve artistic figures in organic bowls. Folklore tales are being immortalized in their typical Peruvian artwork. Out of season, the locals force their products in your hands, hoping you will buy something. An old white monastery with orange roof tiles looks out over a cozy square, stacked with anything you can imagine one can make from alpaca wool. It is hard to reject the generous offers given by the friendly people. It really is dirt-cheap. To some they might come across a bit pushy here and there but I don't mind, it is understandable, for it is their only chance of an income.

In the shadow of mighty snowy peaks, not too far from fabulous old salt mines, ghost villages hold empty narrow streets. Passing these, a winding dirt trail eventually leads to another archeological wonder. Through hills with the greenest fields you will ever come across there lies *Moray*. Pureness of the encompassing nature is overwhelmingly beautiful. Again, in reality little is known about its origin. There is zero evidence of what authorities claim to know about sites like this. Official textbook narratives provide a whole lot of thumb sucking. Grievously one thing becomes clear; if some secret society somewhere does not possess the answers, an incredible amount of advanced knowledge is forever lost.

A minor recommendation goes out to the much-debated city of *Pisaq*, a captivating location up in the mountains. It is discernible from afar by its terraced hillsides, covering entire slopes. If we could only peek into the past to see how they built it at these unworkable heights. On the other side of the river is a ninety-degree-angled cliff, full of small caves that turn out to be graves. A vertical cemetery if you will. How and why were they put there? Who is put there? Mystery abounds. All these places are the perfect preparation for the mother of all ancient sites that will be my succeeding destination.

To give you the short version of a tiring day without a single straight road: it's all very cold and wet. From Cusco to Santa Maria, further to Santa Teresa and later on to Hydro Electric. Just in case you find that a peculiar name for a village, it is the location of a power plant that derives its strength from the *Urubamba* River. It provides power to half of Peru. Tour guides try to congregate uncomfortable amounts of groups of white tourists at the entrance of the narrow path. Passing them as fast as I can it gives me the shivers. Quickly devouring a chocolate bar and three bananas, the hike starts. Walking next to railroad tracks the winding jungle trail ventures deeper into lush vegetation. Here also, mainly infested by young backpackers and adventure seekers from all over the world. Aside from a dollhouse and a night in Paris perhaps, towards the dream of every modern woman: *Machu Picchu*. The village of Agua Caliente, called that way because of the attainable hot springs, is thrown up for the sole purpose of mass tourism. You won't find anything else besides shops, restaurants, hotels and massage salons. It remains an enigma where the people actually live.

After a short night's sleep, I am not granted the warm shower promised to me. Also, a person that made at least five visits here gave me a recommendation to wear long trousers. "Mosquitos will eat you alive!" she said. While the insects are nowhere to be found, temperatures are significantly on the rise. I sweat like a medieval paddling slave. Before the clock hits seven, I take the steep trail up, passing three couples along the way that are leaning against one another, panting their lungs out. Obviously, it is not a contest but I take a certain pride in reaching the top first, on my respectable old age. A month shy away from turning thirty-seven you know. When clouds finally dissolve, I am treated on the view that is so recognizable from the ads on posters and in magazines. Or, for the ones watching television, from their favorite travel show. In total adoration and reverence, I gaze at the competent engineering of generation's past. Hidden away by majestic green mountains as light shines through the morning mist, impartially belonging to the wonders of this world. Ascribed to Inca culture there is plenty of material for a trained eye that suggest a way older ancestry. It comes as no surprise that tour guides are making up history as they go, similar to other locations. The *sheeple* need to be satisfied with prepackaged answers that explain everything so they won't start thinking for themselves. No, that is not what they want. Soon busloads of old folks arrive and scatter about. Flocks of youngsters are standing at viewpoints with their selfie sticks out, smiling at the birdy. That sure takes away the serenity. Around noon, a tube of sunscreen is not a redundant item. It is very applicable as I'm taking a rocky trail towards the Sun Gate. For the lethargic it takes about an hour to get there but boy is it worth it. It's not that big of a spectacle once you are there but you feel as if you accomplished something, in the magnitude of the surrounding nature at this altitude. Your momentous reward is the marvelous view on the glorious sacred mountain of *Machu Picchu*.

Having enjoyed delicious slices of sweet watermelon it is time to head back. Switching vans a couple of times it is still relaxing not having to drive myself for a change, as I am using public transport. The last driver plays several cd's of contemporary Peruvian music. I perceive it as a three-hour long song because it is so insanely similar. Not bashing their culture but this genre sounds like the radio is stuck on repeat. Passed midnight I am back in the jumble of Cusco where a cold night awaits. This time of year is on the verge of flipping into winter. Laying in bed I am giddy from all those hours with sharp-curved roads, without coming across a single straight one.

Two red cats are warming themselves with the first rays of sunshine, chilling on rooftops of plastic corrugated sheets. Watching those cats, snuggled up with their eyes closed, make me realize that little things like this can bring happiness. For a moment I miss the cats I used to own. I was always aware of the lack of any pets while growing up. One of the many things I was dissuaded from by my caretakers. It will not be the only thing being missed today. When I am good to go, I start my engine and leave behind the city with ancient origins, that from a nearby elevated outlook has a strong resemblance to a Smurfs village.

From behind my helmet's visor, scenic panoramas fill the day until the hilled city of Puno shows up. It is situated next to *Lago Titikaka*, the continent's largest lake. At almost four thousand meters high it is exactly zero degrees Celsius outside. The steep hills have a safe vibe but by all means it's not one of the prettiest cities. Tonight I treat myself to a juicy alpaca steak. Also having tried guinea pig and llama, this is definitely one of the best kinds of meat. Snooping around for hours the next day doesn't get me bored at all. In the disorganized center, train tracks are running straight through the daily market that is big enough to fill up a few blocks. Aside from an incredible amount of junk, you can also eat as much as you want. Most tourists however, are here to take a ferry for the main attraction which are the floating islands such as the Uros which is one to write down on your to-do list. Piled reeds with high buoyancy make up the giant inhabited islands. Ingenious techniques of building their reed boats with a perfect aspect ratio, date back thousands of years. According to legend they copied it from the gods who came to visit, which they describe as tall white beings. Who knows if it could have been Nordic Scandinavian tribes who had similar boats. Close-by Taquile is known for its knitted woolen handicrafts, traditionally strictly done by males. Also, when the Spaniards were colonizing they were using the island as a prison, the sneaky bastards. Indeed, inspiring enough to now be recognized by UNESCO.

Towards the Pacific coast is a city that is considered Peru's most beautiful one. With proper grief in my heart I choose not to visit it, on account of being so out of route. So, I cannot write anything from experience about Arequipa. Sometimes you've got to stick by the plans you made. Going southeast I pass mountains with rock formations as if they bubbled up from the very inside of the earth. Birds you won't find in your biology book are skimming across the road, you also find dogs having found their last resting place, presumably hit by some vehicle. High altitudes make it constantly around freezing point. And if it would not be so darn cold I might have indulged myself in all the natural riches of Casablanca. Being nearby the posh city, that is South America's own St. Tropez if you will, this is not the season for a lengthy visit.

If one thing will leave a lasting impression, it is the skillfully dug terraces on mountain slopes, it seems like they didn't skip a single one! As far as the eye can see, everything is made in impressive layers. I can't get my head around the innumerable numbers of terraces, it is truly astonishing and leaves me contemplating about the hundreds of thousands, if not, millions of people that had to be covering these now empty lands at one point in time. How is this not fascinating? But of course it is all blamed on the arrival of the Europeans who sneezed one time and infected them all, pretty much murdering every native on the entire continent. Well, I didn't think so either. The lousiest explanation ever and many scholars count it as proven fact.

Arriving at the border town of Desaguadero, the fist scenes leave a good impression. Everywhere there are stalls with mouthwatering smells of cheap food. Women with beautiful long braids have their edges connected with a decorative piece of alpaca wool. It is crowded as heck though. Too many people dragging too many things around. There are pedi-cabs, market salesman with overloaded carts and overall just an incredible amount of stuff. For a second I am taken back in my memory to India, but folks here are much more friendly and way less offensive. Assuming they are happy, I receive countless smiles from tanned faces with crow's feet next to their eyes.

Crossing a small bridge that operates as the actual border, tinged flags are flapping in the wind. Slowly I maneuver through the sea of people that respectfully make way when they hear my engine. This is how I leave behind the remarkable country that still, after millenniums past, in compliance with the prodigal's tribes, worship the sun in a variety of ways. Including the government, making a tribute to the pagan ancients, who have named their currency *Nuevo Sol*, meaning New Sun.

7

BOLIVIA

Countrysides are hosting decorated fields with recently put together bundles of wheat. In between the greener pastures, the herds of cows, sheep and even alpacas, all graze together. Farmhouses consist of homemade bricks of clay. Complexions of the soil determine colors of the houses, which therefore differ everywhere. Leaving dusty roads behind there's new pavement to enjoy. Not yet aware of the frustrations Bolivia holds in store for me, I am welcomed by a clear sapphire firmament and breathtaking look on an impeccable South Andes range with summits well above six thousand meters, called the *Cordillera Real.* Its obtrusiveness makes me realize how tiny I am.

Not too far from the western border lies the next two sights. Being the icing on the cake in this lonesome wonder world I solemnly chance upon the respected archeological sites of unprecedented Tiwanaku and Puma Punku, clothed in obscurity. When the conquering Spaniards arrived, in total amazement of the magnitude of the cut stone sizes and construction techniques, they asked the presumed aborigines how they built it. The Incas laughed and quite unexpectedly replied it wasn't them who built it, but the gods themselves, thousands of years prior to their arrival. According to the handed down traditions it is even said it was built in one day by a tribe of giants. And who knows? Less than nothing is known about the origins of these places.

Because an early bird catches worms, I'm granted to be all by myself in the ascending layers of mist at Puma Punku. Guards staying at their posts due to uninviting drizzly weather proves to be beneficial. It allows me to cross some fences to investigate uncharted laser-precision hieroglyphs from up close. Letting my fingers slide across the surface I touch the unbelievable fine art that is somehow crafted into the erected gates, meanwhile I photograph all my interests without hinder. Diorite blocks of a hundred tons moved about as if it was nothing. One block is estimated to be around a staggering four hundred forty tons! You probably know those dull images of legions of poorly dressed slaves pulling ropes while these blocks roll on logs. Right. There's no way I'm buying that.

In the nearby Litcó museum you'll find a collection of confiscated statues and artifacts. Seeing all the evidence of carved hybrids it is no wonder that cameras are not allowed, once again, the people pulling the strings diligently try to suppress this part of antiquity. In search of truth we can conclude with certainty that the miraculous dwellings were unmistakably harbor towns. Yet Lake Titikaka is many miles away, and not only that, as of today its water level is also about a hundred feet lower than both sites. Mainstream archeology won't even dare to go here, fully aware it's supposed to take fifteen thousand years for a lake to drop that much. Farfetched as that may seem, I am of the understanding that even if it only took half as much, which is more likely, these cities are very ancient. The way they placed huge hewn boulders of andesite together with bronze hinges was something unknown to this continent, but certainly not uncommon in Egyptian architecture and Babylonian empires, across the ocean. One might wonder why most parts are still not excavated. To put it this way, if there was nothing significant to hide, why won't our government-controlled history books ever mention these things?

La Paz is often referred to as the highest capital in the world. However, not rightly so, since Sucre is the actual capital of Bolivia. Encompassed by snowy peaks, contours of the large city become visible from a great distance. Assuming I will come across the infamous *death road,* a magnet for wannabe tourists, I find out later it's not via this route. Not that today is a good day to proceed on slippery ravines. After I fill up my motorcycle with a type of gasoline only known to this country, I notice the clouds, at these heights nearly skimming the surface, get too heavy. A blinding cloudburst makes rain gear no superfluous luxury. Once in the heart of the specious center of the city it is equally unpleasant and very chaotic as three inches of water gushes down the wavy streets causing a mess. Traffic-wise it is absolute mayhem. It is so crowded I can't even slip between cars as I usually do. My unreliable navigation sends me in all directions except to the right one. Leading me down a very steep slope my trauma of Ecuador comes to mind. As if I smelled it would happen again the narrow street has a dead end! Getting stranded, the air is too thin for the engine to be strong enough to drive back up. When several tries lead to nothing only one option is left. I figure me not sitting *on* the two wheeled chariot saves seventy-eight kilograms. So there I go, walking uphill next to my bike, nimble and cautiously regulating the gas. A wrong dosage can have catastrophic consequences. Arriving back up on the main road my body is overheated from the effort. The altitude causes me to be completely out of breath and somewhat cranky by the unfortunate event. Therefore, the man that approaches me begging for money gets nothing today. A case of being in the wrong place at the wrong time.

With heavy showers still pouring down it is impossible to orientate without a visual on my buddy the sun - a grey sky blocking the view. I've had enough of going in circles. In absence of a properly functioning navigation I simply pick a direction at one point. The darn thing turned the promised two hours into five by now anyway! Everything is soaked when I finally arrive at my hotel in the southern part of the dirty city. I have to say though, even in this weather, the impressive weird looking mountain I get to pass from off a tall bridge has striking similarities with a giant termite mound. I have never seen anything like it. On drier days there are more opportunities to check out the fringes with the cable car system. This remarkable piece of engineering is the longest urban one in the world, stretching almost eleven kilometers.

Not even close to feeling slept in after a night in a saggy bed it's time to visit *Valle de la Luna*. A huge canyon with spectacular mud pillars and deep crevasses. Your retina will rejoice on seeing this one. It has a striking similarity with *Estoraques* in Playa de Belén in Colombia. Erosion has washed away large sections of the mountains leaving behind a multi-colored clay festival – definitely worth the visit. Scientists debate whether there was a sea once that caused all of this. I can't help thinking how easy the Genesis account would explain everything, just as numerous other ancient writings confirm, but that's a forbidden thought.

Having been on the move again, it is an amusing sight how the train goes through the middle of the city in Oruro, passing dangerously close to shops and apartments. While browsing the daily market, I acknowledge that guidebooks are correct in mentioning that it's not the smallest one. Frankly, apart from fresh popcorn vendors, these streets accommodate nothing outstanding. I count myself lucky not attending the annual carnival a few months later, where a gas explosion causes half a dozen fatal victims and about thirty wounded. My body desires rest from the journey but it would be a poor choice to neglect the blue sky; despite the sharp cold it is better to take advantage of the good weather.

The beginning of this route makes me drive alongside the northern parts of the disappeared Lake Poopó, as well as the eponymous labor town, housing interesting ruins. All that remains of this once so glorious lake is a thick layer of salt and forgotten ships that have found their final resting place.

Straight roads eventually stir into the mountains where beauty awaits. The spread-out terra firma is red, green and brown. Both sun and moon are clearly visible, seemingly going in the same direction and everywhere you look are grazing llamas, proving the unusual traffic signs warning against the crossing animals have a purpose. They amuse me. Judging from the little power my motorcycle has it is obvious that I am gaining in altitude. Almost every curve has crucifixes and crosses next to the lanes. Absolutely shocking how many people have driven off the road or lost their lives with head-on collisions. Down in the valleys the grim reality of left-behind cars and trucks, rusting away. In their silence they tell tales of death. Almost at my destination, the sunlight brightens up tall green trees, those typical slim ones you'd expect to find in southern Europe, for instance. Suddenly I'm pulled over by the police! According to their laser gun I was going too fast. These downhill roads in between the orange canyons just ask for it. Because my papers are alright they let me go with a warning. On account of the time difference we are granted an hour more of light. If it wasn't for that, I would have arrived in the dark in Potosí, the hilled city that claims to be the highest in the world. Renowned for its many silver mines – the reason of my visit.

For a negotiable price I book a tour in my hostel to the biggest silver mine around. When it's time to go I forgather with a group of other backpackers. In the company's office, being literally on a construction site, we dress up in oversized yellow rain gear and get to wear a helmet with a head torch. According to our guide, a tiny lady engulfed by a penetrating stench of old sweat, this mountain where we're headed is fifteen thousand employees strong, with four hundred workers alone in the particular mine on our schedule. When a van drops us off I see only a handful of workers; where the rest of all these people are remains a riddle.

The few that are present have one fat cheek where they stow their coca leaves. Ingesting juices from these makes them pretty stoned. Once inside the man-made structure there are these spat out blobs everywhere. Although nasty it can't beat the discomfort of the tunnels that are too shallow to even stand up straight in. At times it is boiling hot with a far from pleasant smell, dust and sulphur grabbing you by the throat. Our boots are not redundant either with thick mud up to our ankles. With tracks from different directions running straight through we have to jump aside now and then. Narrow as it may be, the passing wagons, fully loaded with raw materials weighing up to a ton, can cause some serious damage. After hours of walking hunched in the darkness, all this time unfruitfully reaching for fresh air, it is a relief to be outside again. Workmen are gracious with the gifts we were asked to bring along; bottles of soda and more coca leaves for them to chew on should keep them going. None of these fellows get to reach a ripe old age, they are bound to making ends meet. In fact, they hardly eat anything in order to save money, yet do find a way to be stoned and drunk all day. Being a sucker for a substance smelling like acetone, from the fumes alone I cannot imagine why anyone would drink it. That same substance is poured out over the erect penis of the god of the nether world, hidden away in one of the dark caves. Whatever is left of the bottle is emptied down their own gullets. Yes, they created a lifelike statue of a red devil they call *Tio*, meaning uncle in Spanish. By praying to it, asking for protection and fertility, placing burning cigarettes in its mouth and making blood sacrifices with young animals, it is safe to conclude they more or less worship the thing. By all means, it is not my intention to step on anyone's toes, but it is intriguing how they can be Catholic and so superstitious at the same time.

In the neat center of the city itself you can find perky chapels with huge bells, cheap meals, impressive colonial buildings, and stores that sell dynamite. The second my ears hear the word dynamite I am alert as a gazelle spotting an approaching lion. Almost immediately I buy a stick, together with a bag of nitrogen for a bigger blast. Because igniting as well as owning the thing is only legal in Potosí, I tuck it away in my luggage. Getting on the motorcycle I admit I am rather anxious when I smuggle it out of the city. On the edge of a valley I carefully put the fuse of the cord in the stick and put it on the ground between some rocks. Lighting it up I'm filled with excitement. Coming from a country with massive restrictions I only know about the explosives through old western movies, or coming from cartoons where they blow up stuff with TNT, being slightly fascinated since childhood. As I hide for cover with fingers in my ears I suddenly spot an unsuspecting Bolivian family nearby! Going about their daily business down the slopes they are cutting up a llama, presumably to prepare their supper. Without saying a word, I keep on going. About thirty seconds later a part of the mountain flies up into the air after a bright flash, followed by a loud boom. Sound of the blast echoes throughout the whole valley and my clandestine act forces me to make an escape. While fleeing the scene I can't help to chuckle, I can only imagine what was going through that family's mind, it must have scared the living daylights out of them!

Continuing my way towards the desert, strong winds set up, turning the drive into a cheerless one. Gazing in the distance, I observe another bunch of tornados that are dancing on rugged fields. Not like those insane Hollywood twisters but big boys nonetheless. My uncontrollable curiosity racks me into a decision that is perhaps not the wisest I ever made. The idea sprang up to put this natural phenomenon to the test by running straight through one of them! In doing so I am quickly thrown to the side of the spinning cylinder. Although powerful, it is not strong enough to knock me off my feet. Man voluntarily runs into a whirlwind – Check!

According to my untrustworthy navigation there's a tavern in dead end desert town Santuario de Quillacas. Hitting the first streets of the town, a small group of elderly locals explain how to get there. Upon arrival, the stir-faced owner peeks at me from head to toe as if he is examining me, prior to announcing the place is fully booked. I don't believe a word he says but what can you do? Thus my search continues. Without any moisture in the air the already low orange sun is getting smaller and smaller as it goes further away. Hindered by almost continuous cramps in my knees I drive until I reach the humongous crater of *Jayocota*. Supposedly created by a meteor impact millions of years ago. Personally, I don't find a shred of evidence for this alleged violent happening. What *can* be found, however, are ossified mud blobs. In other words, air had to come from somewhere below, eventually making its escape to the surface. Seems to me we are looking at the mouth of a buried volcano or some sort of a giant sinkhole. Anyway, today exactly eight months away from home and this is the first time I pitch my own tent. How scandalous.

Nightly temperatures make my water bottle freeze solid. When the cold keeps me from catching sleep I marvel at the crystal-clear night sky. Shooting stars are not uncommon but I can still count them. Across the vast heavens appears the purple Milky Way. With my tent partially zipped open it is no problem to see it with the naked eye. I notice the *Ursa Major*, better known as the Big Dipper, arising inverted from the horizon. It is also far larger than I have ever seen in the so-called Northern Hemisphere. Perhaps stars are not zillions of light-years away as they have us believe and much closer to earth? At daybreak I walk over to the center of the crater, where a significant layer of white mushy salt fills it up. Not far from where I'm standing three dogs are chasing a llama who is possibly running for its life. Finding a safe spot, the ice-cold water is almost reaching the shoulders of the animal, which is in a state of panic. The dogs reckon it too thick for them to swim in, instinctively realizing it will drown them, so they turn away. Next to the ring of this perfectly round crater, I find a hundreds-of-years-old chapel with early eastern characteristics, it basically being a cube with a dome, not inconceivable accompanied with plenty of crosses. Having the exact same color as the surroundings, constructed from mud and sandstone, it stands camouflaged. Likely the reason why no other living soul is around to visit. Presumably made by the first Spanish migrants I can almost hear the sounds of the unknown mystique history when I close my eyes. Absorbing the energies, I can sense the former enterprises, lost in centuries, carried by whispers of the winds.

When I start driving it is astonishing how heat of the intense morning sun completely vanishes. It is doubtful my gloves are up to the task. At one point the amenity of pavement is hours behind me, roads solely consist of loose sand and gravel, and my mirrors show a soaring trail of dust tracing my proverbial steps. Nothing seems to be alive in these parts of the world. Livestock carcasses tell the story of harsh conditions. Rocky hills are filled with withered trees and cactuses, only a small lizard dares to show himself before hiding again. More hours have passed without coming across another human being. It can be lonely out here. With so much time on my hands, many thoughts make my head close to crazy sometimes, in fact, it is quite unfathomable where your own thoughts can lead you. In this lost wilderness it takes certain ingenuity to keep acting sane, which is a sport of its own, not giving in to the temptations to quit. Close to an auto-pilot state of mind I keep moving forward until I finally reach one of the greatest natural wonders if you ask me.

There it lies before me, descending from the hills I have a wide view from the foot of the volcanoes to the very horizon: the *Salar de Uyuni*, the amazing Salt Flats! Apocryphal stone ruins of forsaken Inca villages, embedded in mystification, greet me in unison at approaching the former shoreline. Seeing this silvery white arcadia is something the mind can hardly comprehend. The brightness is contrasting with the intense blue sky, I am in awe of the honeycomb pattern over the entire surface, as if inaudible resonating sounds created it that way, not to mention the purity of it all. It comes as no surprise that the masses flock to witness the veritable beauty. While making my way across, the ferocity of the salt actually eats away parts of my motorcycle. For now, I couldn't care less and keep zealously screaming and shouting for joy! It gives the surreal sensation of driving on ice of a frozen lake yet without it being slippery. If you haven't heard of this place, I suggest you Google it. Once you have seen it you might envision that driving a motorcycle on this location, and the euphoria it brings, is a privilege most people can only dream of. And having crossed about ten thousand kilometers over land to get here certainly adds an extra dimension. From thirty-five kilometers away the cactus-covered island of Incahuasi is clearly visible. Even though the nights are freezing it is still a good place to spend your time in. As the sun slowly sets, unmeasurable long shadows are cast upon the plain, it is nothing less than profound.

Uyuni itself is a dusty city with but a few bricked-up streets. Every intersection is characterized by a pile of waste in the middle, existing of rotting fruit and plastic residue of all sorts. For those not having their own transport it's possible to book a tour on a Jeep for three days, where you explore all the major sights. This is an easy adventure for the price of around eight hundred Bolivianos, converted that is one hundred and twenty US dollars. As with most other things in this country this also is a very good deal. In the course of days, I get the necessary chores done. To begin with, at a laundry service they are not surprised to find trousers with my pant legs all stiff from salt crystals. At one of those outdoor carwashes I have my bike cleaned. To prevent further damage, I mustn't wait too long with rinsing the salt off. My chain is checked and tightened at a slow mechanic with an incredibly messy workplace but he gets the job done. Furthermore, I come to the conclusion that I am done with shivering all day, so I purchase an extra thermo layer for the legs in one of the many shops. In my journal

I am quick to write those little details that one otherwise would forget. Such as finding my toothpaste frozen in the morning, not finding toilet paper in any hostel, or seeing posters in restaurants advising about hygiene in sanitary areas. People here still need to be educated that not washing your hands causes all kinds of diseases. Unfortunately, it is not rare for the locals to be infected with polio.

At the edge of the not-so-pretty town lies something rather interesting. For at least a century it is known as the *Cementerio de trenes,* lost in time and rediscovered, a graveyard for steam locomotives. Piles and piles of corroded train wagons, old tracks and warped steel. Very entertaining. Arriving in the morning there is no one there which serves as a great moment to snap some memorable pictures. When I leave after an hour and a half there are fifty SUVs parked at the entrance and three hundred whites have flooded the area! Mass tourism sure knows how to spoil a place.

Cruising southwest more desert is all that is left. Roads are deteriorating as time passes, until the point they can no longer be qualified as roads. In San Cristobal I fill up the tank plus both jerrycans with gasoline, and fill my stomach with a grilled llama steak. I better be prepared for the days of wasteland lying ahead. Diverting off the main road the route leads to Villa Mar. Before arriving in the small village next to a nice piece of rock, I am desperately fighting the deep sand as I am sliding from left to right – it is impossible to drive here. Mind you, this is the official 2014 and 2016 Dakar Rally route, where even the professional drivers get stranded all the time. Go figure! Low gears give the engine just enough power to go forward. Uphill can only be done in first gear. It is downright dangerous and a miracle I don't fall. After sundown I arrive at the hotel where I planned to spend the night; since it is the only one around they dare to offer prices as if it includes two free orgasms. In the now thick darkness, removed from civilization, the situation demands to look elsewhere. The only locals outside, point me in the direction of a tiny nearby village, consisting of a few crappy low-rise blocks. Searching for a place with the lights on it takes a little while before I find an inn. For unknown reasons they are far from happy to see me, when I walk inside and politely ask if they have any rooms available. Almost objecting my presence, they are finally willing to rent me a single bed, yet not without great effort. At least this refuge will save me from the faithless cold that turns everything to ice. Going to sleep with a pack of biscuits takes the edge off the hunger, for I am dying for a big meal but everything is closed already. When traveling you often color outside the lines. Resistant for what is to come, the next day shall prove my expectations to be right.

With incomprehensible discomfort of off-road driving, my own Dakar Rally continues. Making a way through deep tire tracks in the dark brown sand is inhumane. Going forward on roads that have ankle deep gravel, my energy is quick to burn up. Nature fails to push the temperature above zero, little streams and ponds are covered with white ice. Who in their right mind travels here in wintertime? A royal blue sky and outlook on mountains with intensely beautiful red, brown and green colors are the only consolation in these expansive lands, proposing nothing but death. Increasing winds penetrating my scarf make my nostrils scaly, which by now are leaking continuously. Devoid from moisture my lips are hard and ruptured. With the absence of a healthy blood flow my hands turn white and parched. In spite of double-layered gloves, the distinct cold has torn my cuticles, even up to the point of bleeding. I'm beginning to wonder if this was all a big mistake. Raising my head, I ask out loud: "Is this some punishment I receive for my wrongdoings?"

Since yesterday I haven't had anything to eat. I am really hungry, not granting myself the food I need, nor the rest. Every once in a while an all-terrain truck passes, whenever I am out of gas, I signal them to stop; in doing so, never waiting longer than a few hours. In exchange for cash, the drivers stick a hose in one of their jerrycans, of which they usually carry four or five on the roof rack of their vehicles, and fill up my thirsty tank without spilling a drop.

The hardships finally take me to *Laguna Colorada*. Pink flamingos are undisturbed by foreign presence in this very remote red lake. Algae or sediments or whatever the cause may be, seeing red water is definitely a mind fuck, and it is unlike anything I've ever seen before. With dark hills on one side and on the opposite side light desert sands, it is a picture I won't easily forget – a small reward for all the suffering. As days pass by, the intense cold lingers on. I have to pull over frequently to carefully take off my gloves to take care of my hands. Trying to satisfy them with a firm rub I simultaneously exhale a bit of warmth in them. Feeling your own fingers defrost is painful beyond belief. You know, this unsurpassed cold makes the whole vibe of a country different. I realize I haven't even slept with anyone because of it. Except for maybe my right hand one time.

Salt trails through rough red mountains, frozen lakes, cutting winds, and volcanoes with everlasting snow, a distant sun too weak to melt it. Make no mistake, this region is treacherous. Bleak and barren lands have made my cheekbones maroon and chafing. Will my face ever turn back to normal? My cracked lips are bleeding and the first skin layer next to my nose is dying. In fact, it leaves dry and ugly spots until months after traveling.

While my bones remain shivering I press on until I catch awareness of steam coming out from the ground. To my surprise I stumble upon a geyser! How often you have that happening to you? Bubbling pools with an intoxicating aroma of sulphur. *Those bubbles must mean it's boiling,* I think to myself. Upon inspection I cannot withhold myself from feeling how hot it is. Now I go through life as the man who stuck his hand in an active geyser. And yes it was hot alright! But I'm okay, thanks for asking. Moving along through deserts and rock-like mountains, the palette of the Creator mixes it all together, giving a most wondrous outlook. At one point I think I am hallucinating when I encounter people walking in swim shorts while I am wearing six layers – not even being enough. Drawing near to the apparition it becomes clear there are some spas right next to the road. Who would have thought? As wheels keep on turning and teeth chattering the southeast border is finally reached, demonstrated by a very colorful Wiphala banner flapping in the wind, which actually is one of the two national flags.

Security forces exist of but one government employee in a tiny low-grade office in no-man's land. It is almost comical. The good man somehow not bored to death he asks routine questions before putting a stamp in my passport. Having officially pulled it off is something I was desperately waiting for. Literally on the boundary of Chile itself the pavement starts and it looks neat and inviting. Gearing up to continue driving, I give one last look over the hostile yet gorgeous lands behind me, that had me challenge myself day after day. Because my oh my, it was hard and self-seeking! I have no shame in admitting I almost gave up a few times. After a deep sigh I press my lips together, then say out loud with a certain tone of emotion in my voice: "Thank you Bolivia, you have shown me great things, but I don't think I will be seeing you again anytime soon!"

8

―――――

CHILE

A tiny insignificant dot in a huge world, that is one of the feelings when driving in between the majestic snowcapped volcanoes of northeast Chile. Imminently leaving behind the heights of Bolivia, I keep facing inclement winds. Near perfect asphalt is a refreshing change, especially going downhill for two kilometers! Winter sun does not transmit a lot of warmth, if any, but it makes the unending view over the sandy Atacama Desert breathtaking. How the light pierces clouds resembles a real-life Rembrandt painting; there is no limit to its perfection. Mercury rises while I further descend and the first sign of greenery appears in the form of a shrub, followed by more, and not long after the first trees join in. Seeing the earth reawaken after the tormenting hibernation gives so much hope. Upon arriving at the first destination, San Pedro, I decide to spend a few days here. Time to gain some weight with an abundance of fresh bread, fresh salads and fresh pastas around. Do not expect it to be cheap in the touristy areas.

Speaking about touristy things, in one of the many agencies you can book tours for numerous expeditions. Indulge yourself in the romance of stargazing at night in the desert, or take your lover to yet another mesmerizing eroded formation named Valle de la Luna. If you're planning on visiting the beautiful sand dunes of *Duna Major*, with high hills totally covered in virgin layers, don't do it during the annual sandstorms like I get myself into, where the velocity of the winds can literally make you lean forward without falling, like Michael Jackson in his "Smooth Criminal" video. Together with steaming geysers, salt lakes, salt mines and salt flats there are plenty of options.

Soon I learn that driving without a helmet is not appreciated. As I get pulled over by the police in a manner that seems a bit exaggerated with squealing tires blocking the road. Dust arises as a team of four jump out of the car, quickly creating an audience. About a ten-minute Batman-Joker interrogation follows. Hypnotized by my silk tongue, they let me off with a warning. Alternatively, by the grace of God of course. Either way it is a huge fluke, since I'm not carrying my ID, any vehicle papers nor my expired international license. But most of all, as I find out later, I am already five days illegally in the country with an unstamped passport and an unregistered motorcycle! If they had done a check on me, there is little doubt I would have been arrested on the spot. So, time to pay a visit to Customs. They are unfriendly and reckon my case suspicious, yet do not hesitate to stamp my passport. In addition, all that on the day of the 14th of May, my birthday – I'm a happy camper. To celebrate the event, other backpackers and I spend the night having a charcoal barbecue at the hostel. To purchase the meat and supplies, I drive to the market with a gorgeous Australian babe on the back of my motorcycle that I just met. Of course, both of us without a helmet.

Via Calama, I travel west on the map. Formally through the driest place on earth according to multiple sources. Lastly back at the Pacific coast, a night is spent in the dirty harbor town of Tocopilla. Towards it is bizarre how many mines I come across; it must be loaded with raw materials, they haul the mountains utterly empty, doing so with beasts of machines such as the grand Caterpillar 797F. Standing strong on twelve feet tires and using approximately sixty-five liters of diesel per hour. Always wanted to see those things and here they are.

Driving south through sandy plains I pass the Tropic of Capricorn, where the sun, at least in the appropriate season, does not reach beyond. Seawater starts getting blissful cobalt blue around the modern city of Antofagasta and there are so many immigrants from countries to the north as well as Asia, that it is hardly Chilean over here. On a personal level, I feel the need to keep moving because of this. After all, I came to see some rural lands. Moreover, I would always choose a small fishing town over a big city.

By the time I check-in into a hotel in the charming village of Taltal, the so-called brightest star, which in reality it isn't, is already setting, creating an orange gloom across the cloudless sky. Pelicans are skimming the flickering water surface. Fresh fish is being catered everywhere along the rocky coast and rows of uplifting palm trees festoon the dilapidated quayside. Big mansions of the frontier suffer bad maintenance with paint layers peeling off. Wooden lap siding from the houses is not the only thing losing the battle against the ferocious salt, for so is the old seagull covered pier that it is slowly deteriorating.

Continuing with sound of the surf from the powerful ocean, I meet another biker at a gas station in Chañaral. Coming from the very south he urges me to buy electric heated gloves, like the ones connected to his handlebars. Later on, I so much wished I had heeded his warning that I disregard for now, falsely assuming I had been in tougher scrapes. Rocks in the light blue bay are filled with an unexpected surprise. I already thought I heard some strange sounds coming from that direction. Something like barking but different from that of dogs. What a merry sight to see wild sea lions everywhere! Running into those when you least expect it is the icing on the cake. Stretched coastlines prolong to stay rocky until my next temporary destination, which is Caldera, a city not far from the posh seaside resort of Bahía Inglesa.

With my chain coming off for the fourth time my bike needs some serious fixing. Searching online for a mechanic requires wifi and a working cellphone. When I try to charge it in a brand-new hostel I discover the sockets are different, now I have to find another plug first. A little issue like this is not nearly the end of the world, but the longer you are away from home and without the comfort of a quick fix, the more frustrating it can be. Unannounced it is seventy-year-old Rodrigo that saves the day. This former mayor and former governor of a large region knows a guy. While walking together towards the other end of town he gives me a crash course on his entire life story. Frankly I don't remember a word he says, however, the one thing that sticks with me is that his face is badly tanned, while the rest of his body from the neck down remains utterly white as wool. What a ridiculous sight when he lifts up one of his pant legs to show me! Due to his important position, he was used to dress up in a suit, preventing UV radiation to brush him evenly. I cannot help to make fun of him. In the end, my bike does not get properly fixed. Since there are no options left, I reckon it well enough to leave after a few days.

While tying my gear onto my iron horse I meet a bald man with a long beard who is traveling the world on a bicycle. So far, the journey of this adventurous spirit lasted three years already, with no intentions to quit; I envy him a little, knowing I have to resume duties with my company again in a few months' time. Something about the grass always being greener on the other side. During our talk, a lengthy parade is passing by. On account of some Catholic holy day the streets are full of gussied-up youngsters escorted by a marching band. Having sniffed up my daily doses of culture, I start driving along the beautiful coastline, where high waves slam unto the rocks; such a powerful sight. Crossing mostly desert and an occasional sect-like community with but a minimum number of residents, living in trailers and shacks from scrap wood. Those places always have the flag hanging out; I imagine they must be some sort of Chilean rednecks.

Smooth lanes of near perfect asphalt, and tolerable winds for a change, causes me to ride four hundred and twenty-five kilometers in one go.

Reaching La Serena there's still plenty of hours of remaining daylight. From afar, the city's unmissable icon is clearly visible, a humongous cross built on top of the slopes of the old section of town. A concrete wonder if you will. Checking it out in the next few days my luck already signed the divorce papers. Wanting to climb to the top of this vantage point, I am halted by agitated staff of the adjacent museum, apparently, constructional failures make it difficult to get rid of rainwater of the recent typhoon. With the entrance sealed off with barricades, I have to let this one slip. A decent garage in the center comforts me, as what previous mechanics were not able to do before, they can do it here. I purchase a brand-new chain for my motorcycle that gladly receives it. Boldly assuming this one will last for the remainder of my trip, however, soon enough I find out my assumption is premature. Setting up the tent does not even come to mind; I stay at a guesthouse in a mediocre to uptown kind of neighborhood, the proper facility belonging to a friendly Flemish man who married a kind Chilean woman. Engaged in conversation at the breakfast table it is nice to speak Dutch for a change. Especially with their good-looking daughter who is in her early twenties.

Having had a good rest due to a large pizza the night before, I jaunt another four hundred and twenty kilometers, if I am to trust my bike's odometer. Accompanied by the ocean's never ceasing billows on my right-hand side, I keep on giving gas on straight highways and winding roads until Valparaíso appears, the hippie city I end up spending a month in. Marked by colorful houses built on steep hills and an okay beach make up for this country's biggest harbor town. Together with modern and evenly expensive Viña del Mar it embodies a conurbation. Known for its graffiti-smeared walls, a variety of art and of course the somewhat dirty historic old neighborhood, part of UNESCO's World Heritage List.

If you don't have a ragged beard up until your ankles or hair that reaches your knee pit, or some messed-up haircut - partly shaven, partly dreads, whether or not with audacious colors, you don't seem to belong here. Nine out of ten girls have their lip pierced and wear clothes that a homeless person would be ashamed of. Too much marihuana and alcohol consumption provides a surplus of contemporary art in the streets, but that doesn't make you an artist, as most delusional teenagers and young adults have labeled themselves, or baptized others. Nailing one of your old CDs with a rabbits skull to a wooden telephone pole has to be normal nowadays. Oh well, it is probably just me getting old. Aside from all the craziness, you can find good restaurants, talented musicians and friendly stray dogs that everyone in the community randomly seems to feed. One thing keeps me puzzled though: to me it is unbelievable that radio DJs still use prerecorded tapes with fake laughter when they tell a joke. In this day and age that is pretty pathetic. Not overly subsidized it is cheaper than hiring a sidekick I suppose.

At the hostel, a bohemian mansion with a spray-painted facade, I meet two other backpackers on bikes. When they offer to go for a night ride with a local motorcycle club, I have my doubts. Back home I would be slow to get enticed in such a thing, but with certain persuasion, my new friends pull me over the edge. Joining them, I have to admit that driving amidst twenty-five churning engines is an empowering experience! The feeling of being part of a squad like this is very energetic. It is interesting to see how other road users react to our rather intimidating presence. My new friends and I are welcomed as brothers as we hit the road to Laguna Verde. I imagine this location to be a small paradise in the summer. As of yet we are bound to make a fire on the beach in the cold dark night. Me being the only one not speaking Spanish I need little explanation on what their intentions are when a bag of weed shows up. Returning to my bed at five in the morning, this is a memory I will not quickly forget.

Valparaíso is also the ideal place to embark on a discovery-expedition to the remote mysteries of large stone statues on Easter Island. This being a dream of mine ever since I was still an embryo, it is definitely a sacrifice to let this one go, on account of the chance to let temporary pleasures turn into a lifelong commitment, because in spite of the city's vibrant night life, I came here for a reason - more like on a mission.

About half a year ago I met this very intriguing lady who so happens to live here. This mommy owns a restaurant and is half Chilean and half Brazilian. The long weekend we had spent together in the Colombian hills linger fresh in my memory. Arguably not the wisest thing, because later on I get sick, but swimming in the lake at three in the morning with trivial rainfall sure was romantic. When I fall asleep later on the couch, she covers me with a blanket. How sweet is that? Her warming hugs and dark captivating eyes are blazing with affection, and squinting when she smiles, making her so irresistible. However, it would not fit in my life if there wasn't a string attached. She doesn't speak English and my Spanish doesn't reach beyond "*Dondé esta el baño?*" So that's a bit of a problem. Nevertheless, when meeting her again, her arms are wrapped around my waist whilst sitting on the back of my motorcycle, cruising along the beach together and through the hills.

All of this sparks a new revitalizing hope in me. You see, princess-like ex-girlfriends have occasionally accused me of not being romantic enough. Nowadays I do anything from letting anyone accuse me of that again. When she wakes up in the morning and finds white flowers strapped to her window sill, that I secretly put there at night, I know I did the right thing. The next evening, with her son being sound asleep

– at least that is what we hope – we share a piece of heaven when she passionately gives herself to me.

Joined by the spectacle of elevated volcanoes the *Pan American* highway is further leading towards the edges of the earth. New snow has entirely covered the summits. In passing towns like Talca and Temuco, the people's faces are strikingly similar to that of Eskimo's. Who knows how that came about? This route is also the gateway to the Pucón lake district. Somewhere along the way, a cop pulls me over and he is not amused that my international driver license is past its expiration date. If he only knew that I'm not even licensed to drive a motorcycle – I've never taken a lesson in my life.

Having endured day-long rainfalls, Puerto Montt welcomes me with a closed hostel. Luckily, the owner of a guesthouse across the street sees me invectively ringing the doorbell. Ruth is remarkably spry for a seventy-two-year-old lady. Her funny sixty-six-year-old sister, in similar condition, is helping her out at times. Today is such a day as her skinny body places my drenched clothes in front of the cozy smelling fireplace, which warms the living room of the house. From the floor to the ceiling and the walls included, everything is made out of wood, giving it a very natural look. Without asking anything, they prepare tea and sandwiches first, and while they are at it, pour a good shot of liquor for themselves. Incredibly kind ladies.

While my bike is being furnished at a mechanic, I roam the streets. Leafless trees and mostly simple timber houses in poor condition leave a dreary vibe. Not the prettiest of towns but it's still worth mentioning what you can see in just one day. It all starts with an irritated llama crammed into a mini truck trying to spit on me. I actually have to jump aside to prevent that from happening. Another example is the quantity of boozed-up men around, one particular individual can no longer keep his balance. Being three sheets to the wind, he slams six times into a shutter, rips his plastic bag of groceries causing items to roll down the wet street. A fat dude has his tuxedo pants down his ankles in an overcrowded marketplace, shamelessly releasing a jet of diarrhea as if his life depended on it. I stand gazing in disbelief while the majority of people pass by as if this is common practice. At the end of the day, I did not venture here for nothing though. Down at the harbor, the locally acclaimed log cabin antique market is something you don't see every day. But of course, exceeding all of the madness, this shoddy city officially marks the beginning of the well-known and much desired *Carretera Austral*. Stretching over a thousand kilometers, this long road is about a quarter of the entire length of the country, with over a staggering four thousand kilometers! For me, it also marks the beginning of the end.

Resuming the journey of a lifetime on the world-famous road, the freezing temperatures make me realize that it is not a good idea to do this in wintertime – at all. By now, both my speedometer and the board computer are broken, annoyingly not indicating in which gear I am driving. Furthermore, you should know that I'm not a biker who is traveling, but a traveler who is biking; I don't have all the right equipment. Professional bikers have these cool looking hard cases for luggage storage, whereas my backpack is wrapped into two ponchos held together by cable-tied and bungee cords. In addition, where they dress up in leather track suits I am wearing pretty much my whole wardrobe to stay warm and flimsy rain gear to protect myself against the harsh weather conditions. Minor difference.

A small ferry goes from Caleta la Arena to Caleta Puelche. Following Route 7 to Hornopirén to take a bigger ferry, leading to Leptepú. Unfortunately, no sooner than the next day because I miss the boat by thirty minutes. Here I learn it only goes once a day. Thank you horrible gravel road, I write in my journal. Everything goes slow. To kill the time I dress up in toque, a thick scarf, and my boots to walk around town. Having parked my motorcycle in someone's garden shed, my stuff seems safe. A mobile greengrocer gives me some apples for free while we have a chat and standing in his yard yet another man catches my attention. Wearing an orange jumpsuit, he is burning hairs off a giant ox head with a blowtorch; he just killed the animal the day before. Politely asking if I can make a photo, he is skillfully scraping off the skin with a sharp knife. From all the things edible, mostly from things you would not consider eatable, he is going to make a soup out of it. Meanwhile, bright evergreens adorn surrounding hills, in the misty waters lie a handful of fishing boats for the industrious salmon farming industry. I long to enjoy the natural beauty of the area but my fingers almost freeze off, so I return to the comfort of the house with the fireplace where I will be spending the night.

Fiordo Largo's ferry takes me to Caleta Conzalo in the early morning hours. The ferry departs so early I have to set my alarm clock. Having crossed nauseous making waters, Route 7 advances to Chaitén. Endless roadworks are the cause of my tires sliding everywhere in the deep gravel, heavy showers make the way hazardous too. Especially the last two hours when driving in utter darkness in the first period of the evening. I am forced to take off my goggles as they continually block my already poor view. I simply cannot wipe the fog out of it anymore as they are intended for daytime alone anyway. Failing navigation leaves me guessing where to go once more. Knocking on the door of a hotel makes the male receptionist hastily walk down the stairs. Unfortunately, with the notification them imposing prices way beyond my budget. Even for a single night it would be outrageous and a total waste of money. Searching through the dark streets of the city is made difficult by the continuous downpour and lampposts are scarce. Finally I find a ramshackle of a joint and I warm up with a hot shower. Attached to the moldy bathroom is my tiny room with a single bed, and a ceiling so low I can barely stand up straight. My gear and clothes scattered across the room are left hanging to dry. Opposite the street is an undistinguished diner where a lambent red and blue neon sign spoils that they are still open. Weeks of malnutrition has my stomach rejoicing over a big steak. I share a hefty meal with people I coincidently met earlier on, traversing icy waters on the same boat. That night, in spite of the smelly blankets from my bed and the fungal spots on the wall I fall in an apathetic sleep around nine.

Certain traffic signs in Chaitén catch my attention at the first daylight. Pointing out evacuation routes, they warn against another eruption, of the evenly called nearby volcano that shadows the village. If I could only find a way to describe the intense cold, it penetrates my very bones. Frequently I make stops to take my thermos can filled with tea. Yet before drinking, I dip all my fingers in the cup. What a delight that is. Snowy mountains and lots of green follow on this winding route with astounding beauty as I witness frozen waterfalls, turquoise rivers and rock formations pleasant to the eye. A thin layer of ice nails itself to the road making it slippery and dangerous. Driving slowly on snowy places I have to be extra cautious, even when it is not slippery, it lies full of dead tree branches, concealed stones and potholes. Constantly having to watch for obstacles robs me of my much-needed energy.

Having passed several black lakes I find the small picturesque village of Puyuhuapi. It is a cozy entrance with plumes of smoke arising from the chimneys. Remote as it may be, I am told that in the summer season it is relatively well attended but for now it is silent and deserted. Its taverns and guesthouses are more empty than the scrotum of an old stud. This is actually beneficial for me as I never book a bunk ahead. Roaming the dirt streets at night in search of a new waterproof jacket my supper is partially shared with stray dogs. I am powerless against those cute eyes. Back at the room I'm renting it's the same old song, by now it has become a holy tradition to attempt to dry my drenched clothes at a fireplace. Always being a race against the clock since each time I have to wear the same outfit as soon as I wake up. Even when it does the trick like it has done now, ten hours later, it won't be for long.

Fetching my AKT motorbike from out of an old barn in the morning it rains already. That drizzly depressing weather continues the rest of the day. After an hour of rural Patagonia a huge landslide blocks the road. I can hear myself saying "Now what?" Fortunately, the municipality is well informed and helmet-wearing workmen in reflecting overalls guide me in the direction down the slopes towards the shores, where a ferry is provided – free of charge. Distinctively out of season, the crew hardly meet any travelers, let alone foreigners, so they are happy to see me. Hospitable and kind as they are, they serve me a meal and some tea in the well-kept galley. Being genuinely interested they inquire about my sojourn. Me having the same heart I let them share details about their profession, it's fair to say life is hard for them. Salaries and the weather both suck. Yet determined smiles signature their faces and while finding comfort in one another, they are all of good spirit. Especially their ongoing trolling of the captain, whom they comically accuse of being a homosexual. Chilean male humor.

Mostly covered in mist or clouds, the snowy mountains lead from Mañihuales to Coyhaique, the latter being a sort of a South American version of Aspen; amidst rugged wilderness, you will find decadent clothing stores and costly ski resorts. Neatly decorated hotels and overpriced restaurants are not scarce as well as stocked-until-the-top supermarkets, lit up with bright lights as if it were Christmas all year round. My lodge even has a central heating system! Needless to say by now a very necessary luxury. Not that it does not take all night for my clothes to dry, but still. Calling to mind how I started this trip, where I was driving for months in nothing but my island tuxedo, meaning a T-shirt and shorts. How I long for the comfort of that.

Starting the engine after a homely breakfast, I roll without finding any warmth in the open fields outside, sure enough Mother Nature has a bounty in store. Although it is very windy, and unappealing pockets of snow lie to the left and to the right side of the road, when the compass points south it is solely cloudless and sunny. Being out of the ever-dismaying rain is such a huge relief.

Spectacular white mountains in the distance have me steering parallel the green hills, safely in between. Contributing to half a day's journey, the sturdy pavement comes to a sudden halt at Paso Huemules, where my passport receives a stamp without too much effort, except for a minor interrogation and a slap on the wrist. I learn that something went wrong at Customs upon entry after all. Apparently, I was using my transportation illegally all this time! Whoops. Now in possession of the right documentation I am on my way going a few miles down freezing no-man's land. An old boundary stone erected in the high heath reveals my arrival at the border. Hallelujah! Lidded in mud from top to bottom, ten pounds less bodyweight, my backside fossilized and sore, and a motorcycle that's almost falling apart, I made it all the way to Argentina!

With these countries tightly knit together it becomes inescapable to continue the way south without having to go back into Chile first for a brief moment. Having spent a few extraordinary weeks in Argentina, the border crossing of Gendarmería must be conquered.

Distinctive for the area are bronze volcanoes, windy plains and sinkholes in excess. Hardly twenty minutes removed from a hostel, where I had spent the night, my bottle of water tied to my tank turns frozen solid. That should give you an idea of the insane weather conditions. It is a pretty good indicator why one shouldn't be here right now. My thermos can comes in handy; when it is time to pee, I discover my fingers are too stiff to untie my pants. Imagine that for a second. They defrost after pouring hot tea over them. Nowhere to hide from sharp winds, I am aiming for the ferry of Punta Delgada to take me across a fjord-type-of canal, so I can hit the preferred coastal route, *Routa 3*. However, I do not have enough gasoline to make it to Rio Grande. Maybe it is the cold but for some unknown reason I am using more than usual, having burned up the extra power-liquid from the jerrycans, I gamble on making it to Punta Arenas. Well, if it were not for a bitty hidden-away gas station, not even mentioned by my piece of trash navigation, I would have never reached that destination. Hopping into town, I find a simple hotel that includes breakfast. At the end of the day, I sink into a soft mattress, where it takes little effort to close my eyes.

This life is all about balance you know. One day you are lucky, the next day not so much. Leaving early in the morning to catch my boat, it turns out that I'm thirty minutes late due to the time difference! As expected, the boat to Porvenir only goes once a day. Disappointed, I return to my hotel where I check the internet, my jacket still on due to the anxiety. Why did my cellphone not automatically update the time? To my amazement, I learn that every official time-telling page and major online institution is incorrect. None of them display the accurate time. Crazy no? Resetting the time manually gets me on the planned ferry the next day, perhaps the biggest one I have ever been on, amidst the still reigning darkness.

Visible from off the ferry's upper deck, a liberating pink sunrise across impenetrable waters awakes the freezing region. Even the seagulls have their necks tucked away in layers of feathers on their bodies. An orderly harbor village, romantically painted with snow and ice, greets me hello when arriving on the other side. Daylight exposes black volcanic rocks along the coast. Passing a broken lighthouse at the edge and the last shops, composed from local lumber, I start my route with a trail leading through the scenic hills. While traversing serpentine elevations, I detect frozen ponds scattered across, groups of wild llamas run for the bushes when I approach. After ten miles of meandering roads the snow turns into solid ice. Melted the previous day and frozen again overnight. No matter how careful I am, two days before I reach my final destination it becomes inevitable.

For the first time during this whole trip, I fall off my bike. At moderate speed, I smack to the ground. It tears a hole in my pants and leaves a sore knee. My break pedal is bent, a part of the handlebar broken and the worst of all, the chain has come off! It takes all my strength to lift the motorcycle in vertical position again. My lower back hurts instantly, as it never fully recovered from a double herniated disk, an incident that happened many years ago. There is no way though that I am getting back into that wheelchair. With help of the few tools I still have, I manage to get the chain back on, my hands all black, coated in grease. It takes several attempts to get the engine running. By the time I feel recovered to continue, in an unforeseen turn of events I drive about ten yards on pure ice before the exact same thing happens! Again, I smack to the ground deforming parts of the bike and dislocating the chain. Frustration and sadness overtake me, in a sort of an emotional breakdown I almost share tears and convince myself God must hate me for letting this happen. "Why is this happening to me? Why now, having come this far?" I yell to the sky with raised arms if this is some sort of a test. Here and now, it takes all my strength not to give up.

Admitting this is a bridge to nowhere a radical decision has to be made on the spot. There is no option left to backtrack the whole ten forsaken miles to take another route. Guessing the right direction, I am comforted along the way by funny looking birds with huge beaks and groups of pink flamingos. A hard to drive on road, next to a brown rocky coastline, continues through vast deserts where nothing seems to be living. Given it is dry, bleak and deserted I reckon it must be similar to the lunar surface. Diverting from the waters I am pulled through auburn sandy wastelands. Afflicting my well-being, a brigade of antagonizing winds have me shifting gear frequently. Looking up to the west I witness sunlight reflecting from off the dome, exactly opposite the sun. Leaving a peculiar spot of bright light in midair, that would have the layman contemplating. Obviously, I am getting closer to the outer rim, called Antarctica.

Late in the afternoon, far later than the original plan, the barriers of San Sebastian appear as a Fata Morgana in the middle of nowhere.

At Border Patrol things go rather chaotic when at last they allow me to legally exit Chile. I have to gather the limited strength that is left in me to focus on successfully ending this trip. Ushered by volcanic rocks the bumpy dirt road leads to the next border, another Argentinian one. Beyond this imaginary line, I'll have to face the last hardships of the unexplored territory. In the fading of the light awaits the last track of land I have to cross, whatever happens I cannot give up now, with new stamps in my passport I like to believe I am ready. Putting my helmet back on, readjusting my scarf, tightening my gloves, and mentally setting everything aside to reach my ultimate goal; I am getting ready to stand in victory at the most southern part of our amazing world.

9

ARGENTINA

Prominent winds sweep melancholic across unending yellow grass plains, as if they're gently moved by the fingertips of the Omnipotent. Lakes and streams lie eternalized having their surfaces frozen to solid ice. Patagonia in wintertime is no holiday. The primary battle that needs to be fought is against the discomforting elements, the second battle of commensurate importance is against your own thoughts. It requires determination to not let the hopelessness of the climate make you insane. Today's borders mean nothing to the forsaken and lonely mountain range of *Reserva Nacional Cerro Castillo*. Partially snowed-on rock formations effortlessly flow from one country into the next. Compelled to give the cherished Chilean adventures a purpose, I enter into Argentina.

Paperwork is an easy fix at Customs of the border crossing of Paso Huemules. Nevertheless, I spend some time in this remote area, talking to one of the few other travelers. Pleasantly surprised this time it is a Dutch lady who is bravely roaming the world by bicycle. I have to restrain myself from making lame jokes when she introduces herself by the uncommon, yet pretty name of Cinderella. With the both of us finding it somewhat difficult to find the right words in our mother tongue, it's a shrill reminder we haven't seen home for a significant amount of time. When she publishes an article about my adventures and later an interview on her popular travel blog, I am honored with the gesture. Given the ever-increasing cold, she explains how her trip is not fulfilling any longer. Henceforth she plans to turn around and go back north in search of sunshine. Having parted ways, presumably living happily ever after, her ideas are nesting in my brains. Should I also go north? I ponder. In all honesty, I have a hard time enjoying this trip with these temperatures, besides, selling the bike in the capital will be much easier than where I am headed as well. Maintaining my cause with reducing motivation, it is an option that becomes more covetable every day.

Going at a snail's pace through the horrible dirt streets of mini village Lago Blanco, a place to spend the night is presented. It being early in post meridian, however, I keep on going with the intention of making kilometers. Well, next time I will take heed what I wish for since that's exactly what I get, and a lot more than that. It begins gripping with ostriches running parallel to the road. How very exciting! Seeing them for the first time in the wild it takes a few seconds to realize what the heck those fast-moving creatures are.

Impromptu moments like this is what make people want to travel. Relishing in nature's unrefined gifts soon turns into one of the toughest days of the entire trip. A horrendous gravel road keeps shaking me up. Gruesome winds are beating so intense I have to drive in a lower gear to compensate for the speed.

At sunset, the already freezing temperatures literally plummet downward and being at the end of a tiring day it messes with my mind. In an attempt to stay warm, I start screaming my lungs out. Except for a handful of incoming lorries, there is not a living soul to detect. No people, no houses, no abandoned barn, not the smallest shelter, nothing. Not even scattered junk or any type of materials to build something. Perilous clouds foretell the worst to come; putting up a tent without a tarp is not even an option.

Still screaming due to unimaginable cold, my tires suddenly touch asphalt, which is a relief in the now thick darkness. Luckily it's a hard road and not some steep cliff or body of water; my eyes being so tired I would have driven straight into it! Stiff joints of my aching body are making an effort to throw themselves off the motorcycle. In fear of being stranded, it is essential to keep the engine running at all times. Here I am in the middle of the road doing squats and pushups to fight the pain of frozen body parts. Down to my last ration of bread and cheese, I stuff myself to gain energy. A boost is much needed to keep on searching for a place to survive the night. I won't be the first one to die of hypothermia in these treacherous regions.

Back on track, I meet my turn closed off with barbed wire and wooden poles by virtue of the amount of snow. An alternative route has to be taken, nearly provoking a mental breakdown. Scraping the last bits of flexibility together, I choose to be inventive instead, yet not without strive. Sporadically I come across a frozen to death guanaco. The fur coat of the younger and older wild llamas just ain't thick enough to protect them. Hours upon hours, the challenge prolongs where I experience my body starting to give up. Indeed, so much so, my mind has to take over. Solely on willpower, I keep on moving through the dark night, that has no secondary light sources apart from my headlight. Eventually, with an almost empty gas tank, the open arms of Perito Moreno take me in. Visited for its cattle ranches the consoling city has about four and a half thousand people living in it. Resembling an old man, I crawl into the best hotel around, that inadvertently shows itself. Over fourteen consecutive hours on a dirt bike with dead muscles and without food is good for no one. A steaming cup of tea, followed by a well-deserved hot shower, knows how to morph me into a human being again. Having booked a spacious room with a king-size bed, beyond my regular budget, I may finally rest.

Morning light broadcasts a wide cinematic panorama on Patagonia's highest peaks. From the hills, it is astounding how far sight reaches, with the naked eye alone. Over three hundred kilometers southward I have a clear view on the snowy mountains, all the way to Chile's *Parque Nacional Torres del Paine*, and the area of Argentina's El Calafate near the magnificent glaciers of eponymous Perito Moreno. As much as I would love to visit those sights, the weather conditions make it nearly impossible. Not that it would be wise to travel to such an isolated area in this season, at this point I have little faith in my motorcycle and see no other way than to skip it for now, sadly saying bye bye to epic Instagram photo's.

When it is time to get the show on the road again, I am approached by other guests that enquire about the monarchy in my own country. Understandingly, many people are interested in Queen Maxima, since the daughter of the somewhat notorious Zorreguieta regime from Argentina became the wife of the Dutch King. Moments before I leave, I take a peek through the window of my hotel and see others enjoying their *mate* tea, which is drunk by almost every single person in the whole nation. The traditional tea comes in a variety of mug-sized pots with always a thin metal tube in the shape of a pipe, that is used for slurping up the *mate* extract. Mind you, this liquid delicacy is so bitter and so strong that it is easily the equivalent of coffee from the Middle East. After trying it multiple times I have to conclude it is not for me.

Barren lands at Las Heras are characterized by oilfields with those typical pumping machines, jovially going up and down, sucking up the so-called fossil fuels from miles deep. Permanent steppes lead to one of the towns solely thriving on this industry, called Pico Truncado. Having gathered supplies at a local grocery store, I push on, not yet knowing that I will involuntarily return to this place. Off-road driving is interspersed by devastating ribbing and gravel. My suspension and I are given a hard time. It is necessary for my hands to have a firm grip around the handlebars. Flat landscape that resembles dried-up seabed causes a clear perspective on hills, reaching to the far distance. A few good hours off the main road, it turns into a total nightmare, in fact, the only thing of which I prayed it would never happen, especially not in this desolation, becomes reality. Just like eleven years ago, during my journey through Nepal, my irrevocable fate gets me stranded with a flat rear tire! Moreover, just like then I do not possess the right equipment anymore to fix it. This time, in my defense, because most of it was stolen along the way.

Whilst unloading my luggage a thought creeps up. Maybe I should dump this piece of shit motorcycle in one of the few shrubs and catch a semi-truck to hitchhike my way out of here. In hindsight, I swear that if there was a chance at that very moment I would have grabbed it with both hands. As it was, hours pass without any engagement, and forty kilometers to the nearest town is a long way. Bitter temperatures herald the darkness and when evening falls there is no option left than to set up camp and hope for the best. Not having a tarp for my tent, it is a blessing rain stays away. Fear of getting sodden is constantly vexing my gut. Getting drenched here in the outback will cause instant hypothermia, and will lead to certain death. Hearing a car approach at one stage brings more tension than relief when they start firing two shots not too far from where I'm trying to catch my sleep! Let me tell you that if there is anything keeping you from sleep, it is this. Things really get heated when a bright searchlight on top of the vehicle points its beam right at my tent! I was going to hide in a ditch somewhere but now I am too late for that. Who knows who you're dealing with, right? Evaluating if this moment might be my last, I hurl behind my backpack to prevent possible bullets from riddling me. After minutes, a voice calls out from the dark in Spanish: "Is everything okay up there?" Clueless of what to expect I raise my voice and lie it is. From shadows caused by their headlight I detect they check out my covered motorcycle at the side of the road. Mumbling voices in the distance tell me they are in a group. Then as if nothing ever happened, they turn around and disappear in the black of night. I heave a sigh of relief. Due to the flat nothingness, the sound of their engine is detectable for a long time, leaving me unsettled. For who knows if they will return to finish the job?

As the full moon, incorporating a red glow indicating it is a blood moon, makes her way across the sky, the night turns dead silent. It becomes apparent those creepy guys were the only other form of life passing by, except for a curious desert fox here and there. Falling in and out of a light snooze the clock clambers slowly. With the moon disappearing through the invisible sky hatches on one side, hope emerges from the opposite horizon in the form of daylight, followed by its loyal companion, the sun. Previously melted snow, turned into frozen puddles, prove that I wear my jackets for a reason. Pressing the top layer of ice makes it break, in doing so providing just enough drinking water, which I fill up my canteen with. Apart from one piece of bread I had last night I had eaten everything I had. Hands of time keep on rotating until I steadily commute into survival mode. The chances of getting any aid diminishes with nil passers-by up until noon.

Scouting the lands, I wait until the decision is made to be proactive, before getting stranded yet another night. Pushing my bike through soft sand, my luggage tied on the front thus keeping the weight off the rear tire, I am almost instantly out of breath. To lighten the burden the engine stays rolling, but it costs a lot of energy dosing the gas in first gear, my left hand holding the clutch. Fully packed with a non-cooperating tire the whole thing is still heavy. As the day goes by, I have relocated fifteen kilometers closer towards the nearest community. All day without food, my energy level has dropped below zero, as well as mercury in the thermometer. Sweat gushes down between my shoulder blades. I never considered myself diabetic, but I have always been able to clearly feel the level of my blood sugar getting low, or in this case, too low. Exhausted as I am, my body loses balance and dashes my bike to the ground. Aside from my muscles nearly tearing from my bones while pushing it back up, this drop causes the chain to be stuck. Less fortunate than in previous times all my attempts to fix it fail. As if this area is cursed, I spot a horse skeleton only ten yards away! Staring at it for a minute, I convince myself it is an omen, tempting my inevitable fate. Wildlife must have feasted upon it. Not even the smallest piece of flesh or fiber of skin remained.

I am alone and feel defeated to the core. The concept of patience is fleeing from the scene, I have given up. My parched lips are slowly turning blue, my skin goes grey and my eyes set into their sockets. In the beginning of the evening, lying on my back, I gaze at the heavens. With arms stretched wide, moving them up and down, I make sand angels in the brown soil. Everything is so blurry now that I do not even notice covering my clothes in dust. It is a surreal feeling, to perceive that your own body is breaking down and prefers death. Emerging dark clouds make a bold presumption that it won't stay dry tonight. Snapping back into reality, I gather all my strength to get on my hands and knees to unpack and set up camp.

Then a miracle happens – out of nowhere a car appears! Even going in the direction of Pico Truncado. Three forthright hunters, who just whacked a quartet of bad break guanacos, pull over to check why this foreigner lies defeated on the ground. Coming to the rescue, they load up my motorbike on the back of their pick-up truck, next to blood-stained bags with animal body parts. Arraying myself in the backseat with leather interior I cannot believe that I am saved.

Days that follow are unreal. Moved by compassion the related hunters and their families turn out to be true heroes. Within twenty-four hours they have my bike fixed while most stores and shops are already closed, given the weekend has just started. The flat tire is tackled at a befriended tire mechanic – a rusty nail being the culprit in this hapless event – and my damaged chain gets revived by a bicycle repairman. It is amazing how nifty these guys are. On top of that, everything is paid for! Not stopping there, a place to sleep is provided in one of their homes, where I am being stuffed with delicious food. Meanwhile, they even offer to wash my clothes, as I enjoy a hot shower with a fresh wooly towel, smelling like the first days of spring. Completely adopted into this warm loving family their hospitality is unparalleled.

Argentina has her independence day on the 9th of July. To celebrate this event a huge charcoal grill is lit up with more meat than the average butchery. Sitting at a long set table among three Spanish-speaking households, I have the time of my life. All of them being born and raised here they seem proud of their town. As we later go about visiting places, I am treated on the whole tour as if they were professional tour guides. At some sport complex we watch a volleyball match, of all random things, and we join in the joyful festivities of the annual pageant with traditional clothing and horseback riding. Furthermore, we purchase tasteless chocolates at an indoor marketplace with handicrafts and make a quick stop at the adjacent local art museum. Who could have thought my misfortune would lead onto this? Repeatedly insisting to repay them somehow only results in getting more food. Praising their kindness, I think we can all learn from these beautiful people with giant hearts, including myself.

On the other hand, not trying to spoil the fun here but is it possible we all have two faces? A couple of weeks later I find out that right after I left, one of the guys had dumped his wife and four children, one of them being a newborn baby. Only to be with another girl he recently met. What a mystifying world we live in, eh?

One of Argentina's aortas, *Ruta National 3*, further paves the way into the Santa Cruz province. Going alongside something I have not seen since the beginning of this journey, the Atlantic Ocean, indicates that my trip will soon come to an end. Whereas many male backpackers would have chosen to go north instead to check out the pretty girls in Cordoba – at least that is what the country's second largest city is known for – I have other plans. Steering towards my ultimate goal one last sightseeing activity remains. An activity it certainly is, a horrible rocky trail that is way too risky for my completely threadbare tires leads to the fascinating *Parque Nacional Bosques Petrificados de Jaramillo*. As the name might suggest this is a petrified forest. Yielding to the fact that the scenery across the yellow steppe towards it is breathtaking. In addition, there is no shortage of wildlife too; wherever you look, there are large herds of jaywalking guanacos and small bundles of ostriches. For the first time I see skittish behaving maras outside of a zoo, and an occasional badger, neatly dressed in black and white.

Camping in the large park is illegal. Of course, that has never prevented me from doing that anyway, but now I choose wisely. Wondering if the intermittent road signs with bullet holes are used for target practice I'm not sticking around to find out this time. Because we don't want to go there again, now do we? I reckon. A pendulum of grey clouds and possibly present annoying park rangers make me divert to the only campsite in the area, that I didn't even know was here. Welcomed by a shorthaired collie I assume his owners are around somewhere. Having politely waited and checked the perimeter, it becomes obvious that no one is here. Not leaving my side, the overjoyed dog is clearly not receiving enough attention. An urban bus from the seventies without wheels seems to be a fine shelter for tonight. It is corroded and invested with cracks and holes, but man does this remind me of *Into The Wild*. There is even an old bed inside, without mattress or anything, just a rusty frame with a few springs left. Scouting the nearby barn delivers a dusty rug and an even dustier overall, that will have to function as mattress and blanket. Posing on the roof of the bus, I eat my prepackaged sandwiches which have never tasted better. Delighted by a cup of steaming tea from my thermos can, I see pink rays of sunshine begin to stroke the bottom of clouds. The sweet animal, who I nickname Sprokkel, has a fixed gaze on my supper, and I am easily persuaded to share a part of it.

No busy agendas, no constant distractions from my cellphone - all by myself in this outlandish environment. Just a man and his new four-legged friend and an outlook on some wild horses grazing in the far distance through the twilight. The realization dawns this is one of those moments that we as people experience too little. It's times like this that made me want to write this very book. Even if it inspires just one person to go out into this world, my target is met.

I conclude that Sprokkel is not the only one short of attention. Bidding farewell in the morning falls harder than expected. It is crazy how quickly you can get attached to such an animal. Once I arrive at the trees turned to stone the magic show begins, some of the remains of them being one hundred fifty feet long and seven feet in diameter, one can only guess its original sizes. They must have been monstrous for sure! Being the first tourist since weeks, the park ranger is over-zealous in showing the museum with fossilized tree cones. When he starts talking about millions and zillions of years ago I instantly zone out and lose interest. No matter how many lies are fabricated to fit the narrative and what kind of theories self-proclaimed scientists come up with, there is just no way of knowing that. I snap a few pictures and stroll around the lot by myself. Dispersed rocks throughout the dry bleakness have their own charm. Something beyond the shadow of a doubt is the precedent eruption of a massive dominating volcano; it has turned the entire landscape into ashes and sackcloth.

Having spent a night in a wooden cabin in the methodical city of Puerto San Julián, where I forget my favorite pair of woolen socks on the central heating, another half-day drive delivers shelter in the last big city before the border. Although it has to be said that the dirty, grayish, industrious streets of Rio Gallegos are so boring you wouldn't even desire to be found dead here. Or as we like to say back home, you would not even want to breed your dog here.

Resetting myself with some good sleep in one of the best beds so far, I spend the next few days in Chile. Due to the many waters around, basically causing convoluted borders between the two countries, I go back and forth before entering Argentina again.

On the second last day of the entire trip, at the border crossing of San Sebastián, Customs give me a hard time. All my gear and backpacks have to be checked and must go through one of those scanners, looking like a mini car wash for your luggage. Come on really? Do they even know how long it takes to unpack and repack again? Look at all these straps! It is time consuming and in fact, the direct result of arriving in the dark in the slippery streets of Rio Grande, having missed the opportunity to calmly appreciate the glorious crepuscular orange lights. Towards the frozen city on *Ruta National 3* incredible strong winds attack me from the side. It reminds me of when I was driving through a Tibetan desert a long time ago and just like that day, I notice when I look down I am leaning in an angle that would drop me to the ground if the winds suddenly ceased.

At the beginning of the supreme day, meaning the day where I will reach the finish line, all my energy goes to waste. Since the agonizing winds did not subside, the struggle continues. Every once in a while a moment of relief is granted by passing lorries. If I'm lucky and dose my gas well enough, I manage to get sucked along by their airstream, allowing me to drive without effort, being right on their tail. The type of trees growing along the Atlantic coast seem to have died centuries ago, long whorls of moss hanging from wet branches have an eerie apprehension. Like they are drawn shades coming straight out of a Tim Burton book. Ever- attending wildlife seems to have shun away. Who can blame them in this icy feverishness? On the last collinear road, before everything turns to curves, the police, that has barricaded the passageway, stop me. If I have skid chains, they ask. Are you kidding me? "I didn't even know they existed for a motorcycle until you told me," sounds my reply. While making a sowing gesture with my hands I joke that I will sprinkle salt wherever I go. The officer laughs and lets me resume my ride, wishing me a safe one. Luckily, the local jurisdiction made sure there is no shortage of salt on the lanes. Therefore there is significantly less chance of sliding out from under, however, it does have the malodorous side effect of being varnished in dirt from top to bottom.

Getting close to ski resort Tolhuin, all has turned into a white wonderland. Parked cars are hidden by a foot of snow, the ones driving didn't bother to wipe their windshields free, making the irresponsible drivers peek through a small hole they created. Sunshine introduces shimmering waters of the gorgeous reservoir of *Lago Fagnano*. Silvery mountains in the background are contrasting with crystal-clear skies. Capturing the view on camera from off the flexuous elevated roads is virtually impossible. No photo could display what my retina is soaking in. I contently move further, viewing tall pines stand wrapped up in their winter coats of snow, as multitudes of icicles enrich steep rugged cliff faces. Truly nothing can ruin this unprecedented natural elegance - or can it? Fifty kilometers before this journey's ending the unthinkable happens. My chain breaks! What are the chances of this happening now? Drowning in incredulity I get all light-headed. Not only is it broken, it is also thoroughly wedged between sprocket and spindle. You can't make this stuff up. I'm standing there in disbelief yelling repeatedly, "This can't be real!" Yet it is.

Parked next to the guardrail, in a curve, once again I lack the necessary tools to fix the motorcycle. A tribute goes out to the strangers that pull over and provide a helping hand – I would have never been able to fix it by myself on this location. Sent from above I run into an individual that's on his way to a family reunion. With his own wife and children waiting in the car he gets down in his spotless white pants and grabs all the parts with black grease all over! I am quick to say I've never witnessed this kind of kindness in my own country. Another one coming to my aid is a young man from Colombia, who so happens to be driving on the exact same motorcycle! Same brand, same engine size, same everything. The only thing being different is the fact he possesses the necessary missing part that saves the day. Somehow they manage to get the completely twisted chain back in one piece, minutes ago still taken apart into three separate parts to niggle it out from where it was stuck, and put it back where it belongs. Far from ideal but it does the trick.

There we go! Two identical motorcycles with Colombian license plates have eyes staring at us. Cautiously embarking on the last fifty kilometers we cruise together. As if the day wasn't misfortunate enough, the paved road being full of imperfections has *his* chain come off too! Except for minor complications, such as both of our chains coming off a few times, we push on through the slush on potholed lanes. Our final temptation befalls when blue skies turn grey and the gods begin to dump icy rains. Enveloped by snowy mountains everything gets wet. Looking like an animal, I get nervous and excited at the same time, knowing we are near.

And then the moment comes we've been eagerly anticipating. Tall burgundy pillars on both sides of the road with big white letters read USHUAIA. We've made it! Sighing of relief I can't believe my eyes. My body and spirit start to relax into a mode I haven't felt for months. From the very north of the continent to the most southern tip, all the way to the end of the earth. From Colombia to Ecuador, through Peru and Bolivia, across Chile and now Argentina, a total of nineteen thousand kilometers! I am far from being the first one to do this and I certainly won't be the last, but this is an episode of my life that no one will ever take away from me. Echoing my epic tour from more than a decade earlier, it is unmistakably an accomplishment to be proud of. I played safe and I gambled, I laughed and I cried, I tranquilized and wrestled, but greatly embellished I am with new ornaments of wisdom, happiness and peace of mind. And perhaps the best thing of all is that I did all of this without having a freaking motorcycle driver license!

There is no way to sugarcoat it; Ushuaia is decadent and expensive. For those who wish to visit, of course there are plenty of landmarks and points of interest. Boat tours on the historic Beagle Canal along the shores of forest covered hills, challenging glacier hikes towards *Parque Nacional Tierra del Fuego*, or feasting upon the explicit restaurants and stores about. You name it and it's here. Having spent most of my resources, my bank balance does not allow for too many excursions. New lines in my skin, having lost its tan a while ago, show I am tired from all the travel impressions. Having completed my journey, I feel somewhat lost, because I know that it will take a lot of discipline to get back to a nine-to-five job after so much freedom. At the same time, being fulfilled and content, I am not sad saying goodbye to the place. From the money I receive for selling my motorbike I purchase a plane ticket that takes me to Buenos Aires, because you just have to have a selfie with that giant obelisk.

Once there in the nation's capital I try to gain some weight by eating hamburgers every day. Searching for places to eat I go about the city. Strolling sidewalks I almost shit my pants when suddenly three guys with Mexican wrestle masks press their guns to my head. Presuming they are after my belongings I already have my hands in my pockets, with the chance of getting my brains blown out. Lost in thoughts I had accidentally walked into the scene of a movie set! Luckily they are actors, and forgiving enough to let me photograph them as a memory of the fearful encounter.

Hopping into neighboring country Uruguay for a few days, on account of it being so close, I know I have to be heading home to Europe. Besides, I am pretty fed up with collecting my used toilet paper in a smelly bin, instead of flushing it through the toilet like back home, for in most places the drainage system is too low of pressure to get the job done. Thus, in the early days of September, courage is gathered to fly back to the Netherlands, where a wet stormy autumn is waiting for me, as well as an unpredictable cold winter. To this very day I have been backpacking for exactly one year, adding to the list of adventures, with as of yet, a total number of sixty-two counties visited.

171

Always forging plans for future travels there is plenty to research or dream about. But, first things first, since for now I can barely afford groceries. There is no escaping of having to work and save. Actually, I kind of like it like that. Funding yourself gives no greater satisfaction when spending it on new experiences in faraway cultures. Already preparing for the next incredible journey I cannot wait to do what I do best. I think deep down inside I will always be that little child, sitting in the seat on the back of my mother's bicycle, ready to escape to explore the world.

AFTERWORD

So that was it for now. How to properly end a string of tales anyway? To know the last page of these writings is certainly not the end of the story. One might argue if a story ever truly ends in the first place. If only people keep reading and talking about it, it may actually live forever.

Stories are created by dreamers, and daring to dream involves risk. Start your own search for true happiness and begin today. Throw your television set out of the window in order to put a halt to the lies and indoctrination. Set yourself free from the utter nonsense that kills brain cells and leaves you bitter and spiritually poor. Go easy on eating pork because it's ruining your body and infects your soul, and while you're at it, try to hold back on the E-numbers as well. It might be a major change.

You don't have to be a tree-hugging loony to take care of yourself. Don't be afraid of rejection or kicking useless friends out of your life who aren't real ones to begin with. What do you have to lose? Nothing. What can you gain?

Precious time to invest in yourself and things that matter. If done in a natural way, working out in the gym will actually make you a better person.

And for the love of God, make up your own ideas instead of letting others decide for you. Sitting home depressed, watching your life go by, or going to waste, is a destructive suicidal thing that drags you down into depths rather avoided. People who had a long and fruitful life hardly regret the things they did, yet they do regret the things they didn't do.

Being born into a family that never believed in me, where enthusiasm was mocked, creativity ridiculed and fantasy scoffed at, it was a long and heavy journey to break free from all that negative energy, for the lack of a better term.

When I was about ten years old I hitchhiked for the first time. That day I drifted from home quite a bit, strolling along dense reed shorelines of a big lake. As usual, my eyes were set to find bird skulls and real treasures, so much so this particular time that I didn't notice massive thunderclouds rolling in.

When lightning began their incursion in the perimeter, I realized there was nowhere to hide in the unprotected open fields. At a nearby highway I put my little unsuspecting thumb up in the hope to escape the armageddon upon me. Soon enough, in fact moments before the weather would turn savage, a couple pulled over in the smallest car you've ever seen. Behind the wheel sat a man with a long dark ponytail, silver rings in both ears, a black leather vest and his arms tattooed. Next to him an old lady with long grey hair, looking like a stereotypical witch. It took a few seconds for my curiosity to prevail over the hesitation. Seldom did I meet such lovely people though, a bit weird perhaps, but lovely.

Once home, my parents were clearly more angry I got into a stranger's car than relieved that I'm back safely. Not a sign of concern nor compassion. It's because of this reaction I don't venture hitchhiking even a single time in the following fifteen years.

Every once in a while you find a real home in unsuspected corners. For example, back in the early fall of 2003 I happened to be in the Swiss country side, bordering France. Leaving wooden mini-villages behind I am getting ready to climb a certain mountain at the foot of the Alps. It seems a well-considered thought to ask to fill up my water bottles at a small farmhouse next to fenced-in horses. Noticing my stuttering while trying to find the right words in French the lady of the well-maintained house takes the initiative to shift to German, a language we both happen to speak quite decent when required. Chatting away about my planned solo ascension and the reason why I am dressed in a camouflaged army uniform (for me and my friends loved to have survival weekends in the woods) it turns out her daughter had communion that very morning. It is Sunday and the whole family just came back from church. Now seated at a long table with spotless white sheets, cutlery of real silver and a surplus of traditional local dishes. Although feeling a bit awkward and out of place I accept her spontaneous invitation to the celebration. Shy children observe the intruder from across the table until the first one approaches. It doesn't take very long to be surrounded by them, all wanting to take a picture with me.

One delicious lunch later the lady of the house starts off a serious conversation, leading up to her asking me about my dreams. By now it's just the two of us in a different part of the beautiful spacious overgrown garden. Unknowingly being three years away from the actual event, I open up and share I am going to Tibet to climb Mount Everest. This is on my agenda and nothing can make me deviate from this goal.

Completely contrary to the patronizing responses I'm used to receive she says the following thing that I will carry in my heart for the rest of my life: "Send me a message when you're there," meanwhile writing her contact information on a piece of paper. Wait, what? From the undeniable determination in her voice I know instantly she has put all her faith in me. Almost choking up I detect not even the slightest glimmer of cynicism. She recognized the passion in my eyes. Perhaps for the first time in my life I feel as if someone really believes in me and my capabilities. Bizarre to get such encouragement from a total stranger.

Speaking about reaching goals, a prominent one is aiming for the opportunity to inspire others with my story.

Hopefully you enjoyed reading my comprised endeavors, and join me in continuing where I left off in the next upcoming volume! Whoever you are, wherever you are, in any given time, in any given place, embrace the unknown and always be good to go!

TRAVEL ADVICE AND TIPS

Whether you go backpacking with your best pal, a group of friends, or completely solo - how do you prepare for such a trip? And once going, what to look out for?

For your consideration, in this section I will tell you some things that, figuratively speaking, you should carry along with you while going abroad. Although some points that I address might seem logical, and others over-the-top, this is my advice to you because it is easy to forget things.

It is up to you what to do with it. Do you think you are good to go?

Let's start with the most obvious one. Check the expiration date on your passport, or, get yourself a passport in the first place. In some countries you're not allowed entry if your document is less than three months valid. Moreover, getting a new one from abroad can be a painful process, therefore, it is better to carry one with enough space for stamps, and one that allows you to be flexible, in case you want to prolong your stay.

Assuming you checked if a visa is necessary, prior to embarking on your journey, once you are in a foreign country, it is nice to know where your embassy is located. Write down the phone number and address, and keep it with you at all times, because you just never know nowadays. And while you're at it, check for the local emergency number as well; better be safe than sorry.

Going on a far-away budget trip, you will need a good backpack instead of dragging a suitcase through the mud uphill. Even if you don't have much to spend, don't go stingy on choosing a backpack; for this can be all the difference. Don't forget that your whole life is stored in this piece of fabric, it will be your walk-in closet and it will host your toiletries and portable bed, not to mention important documents or electronics. Take one that is tough, lightweight, adjustable, and has comfortable shoulder straps.

Everyone likes to be liked, and I know that most of us believe that people are inherently good. Unfortunately, the ugly truth is that this is not the case everywhere you go. If you are at your hostel or hotel, or know people a bit longer, you can be trusting, however, if you step out from the airport or take a taxi, or enter a store, never tell locals that it is your first time in the country. And believe me, whenever there is money involved, they will ask you this question. I understand it goes against your nature to tell a lie, but to strangers it is better to say it is your third time, or you visit annually, because scammers are everywhere.

If you have traveled over sixty countries, like I did, it should be clear that it is impossible to learn the language of everywhere you go. Having said that, even if you move somewhere for only a month, it is amazing how many doors will open if you speak some of the language, hence, before you go, learn some basic words or sentences. Additionally, with this you will show interest and respect in other peoples culture, which, first of all, will always be appreciated, and second, will be very helpful for yourself to understand things.

In spite of where you were born, if you are reading this book and are able to travel the world, you are probably used to a certain type of living, and sometimes it can be hard to let go of our general comfort. Even so, leaving the so-called West I urge you to support local businesses, in stead of getting a quick-fix at nice looking supermarkets with A-brands, chain stores, or fast-food restaurants. Of course they have the right to exist, yet often a place is ruined by (too many) foreign investors with local people suffering. It's just something to think about.

Even when you are not materialistic, or consider yourself a minimalist, people are natural collectors. We like stuff. This attribute is not helpful when traveling for a few months – or longer. I suggest you divide your belongings in two backpacks, a big one for on your back, and a smaller one which you can carry at the front, a daypack. The last mentioned is especially handy once you're settled and like to check a city or go on a small hike. Also, don't bring unnecessary things, you need far less than you imagine. Think about what climate you will be in, but never bring too much; I promise you that you will regret it.

Something you can't afford to not take with you at all times is cash. Especially US dollars. Owning a credit card is a bad idea anyway in my opinion, and your debit card will be refused here and there, if there is an ATM available in the first place. You can hide some money in a money belt or in your socks, shoes, or clothes, or even choose to carry a second wallet or purse with you, a reserve; the one you can give away in case you get mugged, with but a little amount in it.

Last but not least:

- Buy a wall plug with differing outlets.
- Drink bottled water.
- Wear sunscreen.
- Change your socks frequently (seriously).
- Bring a tool knife.
- Keep a journal.
- Don't be obsessed with your phone.
- Meet with locals.

- Take a rapidly drying towel with you.
- Also pills for diarrhea (thank me later).
- Don't forget that some people are less fortunate.
- Send a postcard to your grandparents.
- Be kind to animals.
- Not everyone appreciates when you stick your camera lens right in their faces.
- Don't rush things.
- Respect the local law.
- Bring some giveaways that represents your own culture or country.
- Do some voluntary work if you have the time.
- Have fun but don't trust anyone.
- Remember that not everyone wants to hear you play your instrument.
- When poor people show hospitality without expecting anything in return, do Something in return anyway.
- Adapt to your host country's culture to a certain degree if possible.
- Beware of pickpockets at all time.
- The cheap mosquito repellents are just as good as the expensive ones.
- Vaccinations are overrated; in worst case scenario everything can be treated afterwards.
- Don't complain; it was your choice to go traveling.
- Get to know the exchange rates.
- Don't stay too connected with home front and learn to let go, be in the moment and enjoy.
- Bring hand sanitizer.
- Take a waterproof pouch with you to keep the most valuable things away from moist.
- Best not to assume anything.
- Milk comes in a bag instead of a carton.

- Be patient or start learning.
- For the guys; wear a freaking condom.
- For the girls; don't go out alone at night.
- For the non-binaries; whatever, I guess, you know best.
- Different does not mean less good.
- Please consider your fellow backpackers in dormitories.

Or (and perhaps this is the best advice) completely ignore anything you just read and figure it all out for yourself!

Happy travels!

THANK YOU

Dear Reader

Having written *Beyond the Equator* means a lot to me, and I feel grateful for the many positive comments I have received so far, also for its predecessor Breaking Free.

I would greatly appreciate it if you could possibly post a short review.

Thanks a lot in advance!
Jeffrey

* * *

A special thanks goes out to my to my Pocahontas.
Even though our roads lead to opposite cardinal directions, this cowboy will always be thankful for all you've done.

* * *

ABOUT THE AUTHOR

So far Jeffrey Vonk has travelled over 60 countries, and authored three books, two of which from the series of *Good to Go!*

Coming from a Dutch working-class family, he started out as a carpenter, got himself certified as an outdoor sports instructor and made it to university through pure determination.

Although Jeffrey loves being at home writing, realizing his dreams of tasting new cultures is what he does best. Ever-yearning for raw adventure, the icy trails of Mount Everest are not unknown to him, as well as meeting up with members of Hezbollah in the Middle East, or experiencing a Peruvian jail cell from the inside.

Traversing the arena of the world on foot, motorcycle, or even horseback, being on the road is the sole passion of his heart.

Getting himself into trouble at times, as a modern-day Marco Polo he follows in the footsteps of the first true explorers.

Do you wish to know where he sets his foot next?

www.ingramcontent.com/pod-product-compliance
Lightning Source LLC
Chambersburg PA
CBHW060139150626
46550CB00015B/1907